contents

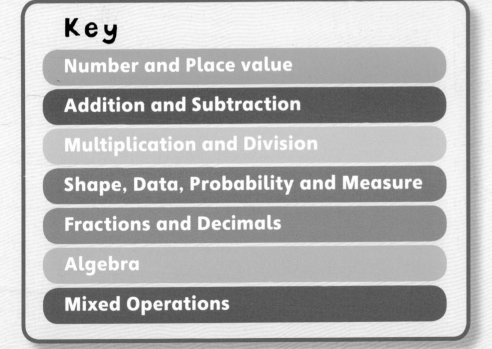

Key

Number and Place value

Addition and Subtraction

Multiplication and Division

Shape, Data, Probability and Measure

Fractions and Decimals

Algebra

Mixed Operations

How to use this book

The first page of each section will have a title telling you what the next few pages are about.

Read the instructions carefully before each set of questions.

Some pages will show you an example or model.

Sometimes a character will give you a tip.

Adding and subtracting decimal numbers

Perform these decimal subtractions.

$$27 \cdot 63 - 14 \cdot 85 = 12 \cdot 78$$

Remember to jump to the next whole number, then the next multiple of 10, then on to the final number.

Try not to confuse decimal jumps and whole numbers.

1. $38 \cdot 43 - 27 \cdot 82 = \square$
2. $26 \cdot 55 - 18 \cdot 73 = \square$
3. $35 \cdot 27 - 26 \cdot 13 = \square$
4. $43 \cdot 49 - 37 \cdot 77 = \square$
5. $59 \cdot 58 - 46 \cdot 05 = \square$
6. $63 \cdot 32 - 54 \cdot 88 = \square$
7. $65 \cdot 72 - 48 \cdot 69 = \square$
8. $72 \cdot 08 - 66 \cdot 45 = \square$
9. $84 \cdot 35 - 71 \cdot 63 = \square$
10. $50 \cdot 94 - 38 \cdot 17 = \square$
11. $75 \cdot 49 - 69 \cdot 36 = \square$
12. $94 \cdot 01 - 79 \cdot 26 = \square$

THINK Draw a Frog subtraction that involves three jumps and ends on 30. The first jump should be a 2-place decimal and the second jump is less than 10.

I am confident with performing subtractions of 2-place decimal numbers.

62

Complete these calculations using mental methods.

1. $16 \cdot 8 + 4 \cdot 12 = \square$
2. $30 \cdot 54 + 7 \cdot 41 = \square$
3. $24 \cdot 63 - 8 \cdot 2 = \square$
4. $36 \cdot 58 - 4 \cdot 35 = \square$

Use column addition to perform these calculations.

5. $\begin{array}{r} 45 \cdot 76 \\ 18 \cdot 21 \\ \hline \end{array}$
6. $\begin{array}{r} 54 \cdot 84 \\ + 41 \cdot 62 \\ \hline \end{array}$
7. $\begin{array}{r} 34 \cdot 28 \\ + 17 \cdot 37 \\ \hline \end{array}$
8. $\begin{array}{r} 37 \cdot 57 \\ + 25 \cdot 62 \\ \hline \end{array}$

Use Frog to perform these subtractions.

9. $7 \cdot 42 - 3 \cdot 86 = \square$
10. $11 \cdot 33 - 4 \cdot 79 = \square$
11. $12 \cdot 67 - 9 \cdot 73 = \square$
12. $24 \cdot 52 - 18 \cdot 69 = \square$

THINK Cat has used Frog to solve a subtraction but she thinks she has got the wrong answer! Help her by finding her mistake and then showing her how to solve it correctly.

$$5 \cdot 4 - 1 \cdot 78 = 5 \cdot 6$$

I am confident with using different methods to solve decimal additions and subtractions.

63

THINK questions will challenge you to think more about the maths on the page.

Each area of maths has its own colour.

Choose a traffic light colour to say how confident you are with the maths on the page.

Reading and writing 7-digit numbers

Write each of these numbers in figures.

1 Four million, three hundred and forty-eight thousand, nine hundred and twelve

2 Nine million, six hundred and fifteen thousand, two hundred and fifty-seven

Put > or < between these pairs of numbers.

3 4 633 231   8 633 885

4 3 467 333   3 579 164

5 6 676 001   6 612 002

6 1 552 817   1 550 994

Write each set of numbers in order from smallest to largest.

7 8 506 253   3 740 100   1 896 741

8 5 245 122   989 738   883 689

9 7 100 003   7 502 257   4 997 978

10 3 950 314   3 509 314   3 590 314

THINK A number in the millions has three 7s and four 0s. What are the largest and smallest numbers that it could be?

○
○

I am confident with reading and comparing 7-digit numbers.

Write each of these numbers in figures.

1 Seven million, two hundred and forty-two thousand, six hundred and thirteen

2 One million, six hundred and twelve thousand, one hundred and one

3 Three million, nine hundred and forty thousand, eight hundred and twelve

4 Six million, six hundred and one thousand, two hundred and nine

5 Four million, four hundred and eighteen thousand, nine hundred

6 Nine million, seven hundred and sixty-seven thousand and fifty-seven

7 Choose any two of the numbers from above and compare them using < or >. Do this four times.

Do you always have to read the whole number to know if it's bigger or smaller?

Write each set of numbers in order from smallest to largest.

8 6 500 003   650 004   6 005 003   6 050 003

9 5 100 673   5 502 257   5 997 978   5 896 741

10 4 005 122   50 738   450 689   4 050 741

11 7 952 314   7 959 314   7 950 314   7 959 701

 THINK   The digits of a number in the millions are a sequence of numbers decreasing in 1s. The sum of the digits is 35. What is the number?

● ○ ○ ○ **I am confident with reading and ordering 7-digit numbers.**

Write each of these numbers in figures.

1. Nine million, two hundred and one thousand, six hundred and six

2. Five million, eight hundred and sixteen thousand and nine

3. Three million, forty-four thousand, eight hundred and thirty-four

4. Seven million, six hundred and fifty thousand and seventy-nine

5. Four million, three thousand, nine hundred and eight

6. Eight million, five hundred and fifty-seven

7. Two million and forty

8. Six million, ten thousand and ten

9. Choose any two of the numbers from above and compare them using < or >. Do this four times.

Write each set of numbers in order from smallest to largest.

10 3 700 073	373 007	3 070 077	3 070 300
11 9 100 001	9 101 001	9 101 010	9 100 100
12 8 765 122	99 765	988 765	8 776 543
13 6 666 667	6 666 766	6 676 666	6 666 666

 What number is exactly halfway between 1 and 1 million and 1?

I am confident with reading and ordering 7-digit numbers.

Complete these calculations using mental strategies.

1. $7\,006\,004 + 20\,000 + 300 =$ ☐

2. $3\,840\,050 + 6000 + 300 + 7 =$ ☐

Look carefully! Only part of each number will change.

3. $8\,994\,738 - 30\,000 - 4000 - 3 =$ ☐

4. $6\,231\,956 - 100\,000 - 20\,000 - 30 =$ ☐

5. $4\,121\,622 + 600\,000 + 3000 + 4 =$ ☐

6. $8\,035\,562 - 5\,000\,000 - 20\,000 - 60 =$ ☐

Subtract the 4 from each number!

$5\,463\,210 - 400\,000 = 5\,063\,210$

7. $7\,184\,639$

8. $8\,241\,876$

9. $2\,491\,068$

10. $1\,777\,040$

11. $3\,552\,402$

12. $6\,249\,899$

Write the largest 7-digit number possible where each digit is one more or one less than its neighbouring digits. Now write the smallest.

● I am confident with understanding place value in
○ 7-digit numbers.
○

7

1. 3 624 572 + 20 106 = ☐

2. 9 572 156 − 3 200 030 = ☐

3. 3 129 672 + 420 200 = ☐

4. 5 467 156 − 1 040 003 = ☐

5. 4 104 783 + 50 011 = ☐

6. 6 663 984 − 1 000 750 = ☐

7. 8 372 978 − 210 400 = ☐

Subtract the 4s and the 2s from each number!

 4 304 328 − 4 000 000 − 4 000 − 20 = 300 308

8. 7 402 924

9. 4 223 864

10. 2 347 256

11. 3 421 248

12. 2 142 256

13. 5 444 242

 Write a 7-digit number that is a palindrome (reads the same backwards as forwards). No digit should be smaller than 7. Make sure you use different digits for the 100s, 10s and 1s.

● I am confident with understanding place value in
○ 7-digit numbers.
○

8

Write the value of the 3 in each number.

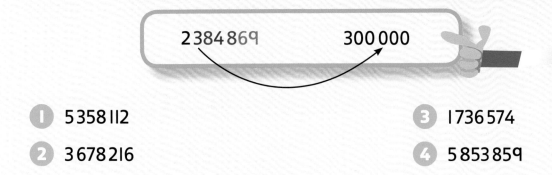

2 384 869   300 000

1 5 358 112

2 3 678 216

3 1 736 574

4 5 853 859

5 Choose a number, then choose a digit and write its value.

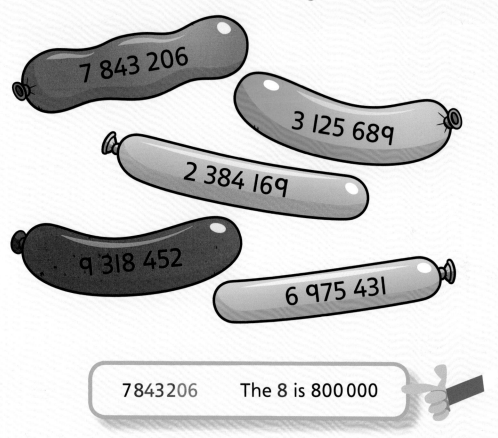

7 843 206

3 125 689

2 384 169

9 318 452

6 975 431

7 843 206   The 8 is 800 000

6 Now write the five balloon numbers in order from smallest to largest.

What number is exactly halfway between 999 999 and 2 million and 1?

Place each number on a number line and round it to the nearest million.

First draw a number line starting at the million before and finishing at the million after.

2 384 689

```
2 000 000                    3 000 000
```

Now label the halfway mark and use it to help you put your number on the line

```
2 000 000        2 500 000        3 000 000
        2 384 689
```

Finish off by writing what million the number rounds to.

2 384 689 rounds to 2 000 000

1. 7 233 563
2. 3 811 642
3. 6 582 684
4. 3 497 992

5. 4 268 773
6. 8 099 486
7. 5 583 532
8. 9 646 101

THINK   If a line is drawn from 1 million to 10 million, how many lines would be needed to mark all of the 100 000s?

I am confident with reading and comparing place value in 7-digit numbers.

Subtracting large numbers

Perform these subtractions.

1
```
   8274
−  6421
```

6
```
   61 728
−  37 254
```

2
```
   97 736
−  74 609
```

7
```
   53 626
−  21 894
```

Choose the best method to solve each problem.

3
```
   86 736
−   9 423
```

8
```
   8912
−  3478
```

4
```
   9382
−  7641
```

9
```
   91 332
−  24 609
```

5
```
   86 737
−   2 808
```

10
```
   82 421
−  34 771
```

 THINK Choose one of your subtractions.
Use addition to check your answer.

○
○○○ **I am confident with subtracting 4-digit and 5-digit numbers.**

Perform these subtractions using the column method.

1   583 973
      − 275 895

2   245 583
      − 153 609

3   859 364
      − 722 785

4   957 736
      − 559 809

5   3 685 142
      − 826 864

6   716 341
      − 589 932

7   8 802 572
      − 3 241 894

8   3 563 026
      − 856 679

9   9 133 628
      − 5 674 956

10 7 307 077
      − 949 838

Make sure you put each digit in the correct column.

 THINK   Using the digits 0–9, write a 5-digit subtract 5-digit calculation that gives the smallest possible answer.

I am confident with subtracting 6-digit and 7-digit numbers.

12

Perform these subtractions. Choose the best method for each one.

1 79 186 – 78 897 = ☐

7 677 565 – 74 290 = ☐

2 48 678 – 41 980 = ☐

8 59 142 – 48 936 = ☐

3 32 847 – 12 347 = ☐

9 95 728 – 14 973 = ☐

4 52 186 – 48 875 = ☐

10 648 562 – 40 060 = ☐

5 64 167 – 48 291 = ☐

11 94 164 – 77 409 = ☐

6 86 343 – 20 012 = ☐

12 267 352 – 59 194 = ☐

 What number must be subtracted from 111 111 to give an answer of 99 999?

Perform these subtractions. Choose your method carefully.

1 364 213 – 24 314 = ☐

2 772 847 – 89 674 = ☐

3 867 343 – 260 013 = ☐

4 522 462 – 486 875 = ☐

5 804 251 – 629 453 = ☐

6 654 167 – 434 100 = ☐

7 372 847 – 269 949 = ☐

8 965 708 – 214 973 = ☐

9 509 142 – 438 936 = ☐

10 6 748 562 – 401 060 = ☐

11 6 267 302 – 896 137 = ☐

12 9 944 164 – 747 409 = ☐

Are the numbers close together, can they be rounded or would column addition be best?

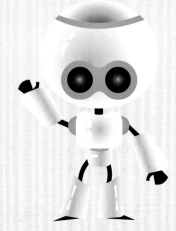

 Using just the digits 0 and 1, create a 6-digit subtract 5-digit calculation with an answer of 99 109.

I am confident with subtracting from 6-digit and 7-digit numbers.

2- and 3-place decimal numbers

Divide each number by 100. Find a number that matches your answer in the box.

> 343 135
>
> 343 135 ÷ 100 = 3431·35 = c

1. 45·7
2. 47 137
3. 7135
4. 573 444
5. 457
6. 23·1
7. 471 370
8. 23 100
9. 34 313

a) 0·653
b) 573·444
c) 3431·35
d) 343·13
e) 2·31

f) 7·135
g) 471·37
h) 71·35
i) 5734·44
j) 0·457

k) 0·231
l) 4·57
m) 231
n) 4713·7
o) 45·7

Solve these problems.

10. How many months are there in a century? In a millennium? How many weeks are there in a century? In a millennium?

11. A car costs 47p per mile to drive. How much will it cost to drive the car 100 miles? How much to drive 1000 miles?

12. James saved £15 per week for 100 weeks. How much did he save? How much would he have saved after 2 years?

THINK Work with your partner to choose a number. You multiply it by 10. Your partner multiplies it by 100. How many more multiplications must you do than your partner to get to 6 million?

I am confident with multiplying and dividing by 10, 100 and 1000.

Write < or > between each pair of numbers.

1. 3·41   3·5
2. 7·01   7·13
3. 7·01   6·99
4. 9·04   9·21
5. 3·6   3·58

6. 4·62   4·26
7. 4·5   4·32
8. 8·12   8·2
9. 3·347   3·374
10. 2·109   2·099

Write a number that falls between each pair.

11. 4·2   4·185
12. 8·9   8·931
13. 2·17   2·117
14. 7·10   7·011
15. 3·64   6·432

16. 3·06   3·107
17. 6·0   5·807
18. 5·48   5·845
19. 6·2   6·203
20. 1·01   1·101

 Write 3 different distances between 3 km and 4 km, each with 3 decimal places. Write them in order from shortest to longest.

○ I am confident with ordering and comparing 2- and
○ 3-place decimal numbers.

Think of a number that falls between each pair. Write all three in order from smallest to largest.

1 2·9   2·648

2 3·01   3·101

3 6·7   6·95

4 5·1   4·23

5 8·6   8·02

6 9·341   9·56

7 3·491   3·55

8 2·8   2·897

9 4·07   4·6

10 3·009   3·08

11 8·31   8·6

12 5·67   5·609

13 8·773   8·8

14 6·235   6·24

15 7·042   7·4

16 1·482   1·478

3   4   5   6

 THINK
How many numbers between 3 and 4 can you make using these digits? The numbers can have 1, 2, or 3 decimal places. How can you prove that you have found them all?

I am confident with ordering and comparing 2- and 3-place decimal numbers.

17

Follow these instructions.

6·072   3·199   6·27

3·201   3·12

3·9   6·29   6·02

1. Choose two numbers from above and write < or > between them. Do this four times.

2. Choose two numbers from above and think of a number that falls between them. Write all three in order from smallest to largest. Do this four times.

3. Write all eight numbers from above in order from smallest to largest.

Complete these challenges.

4. Use the digits 3, 4, 5 and 6 to write two different decimal numbers as close to the number five as you can. One number should be less than five and the other should be more than five.

5. Work out how far away each number is from the number five.

6. Use the digits from question 4 to write the next two closest numbers to five.

7. Work out how far away each number is from the number five.

8. Work out the difference between the numbers in the answer to question 5 and the answer to question 7. What do you notice?

● ○ ○ I am confident with ordering and comparing 2- and 3-place decimal numbers.

Equivalent fractions and decimals

Write the decimal equivalent for each of these fractions. Use a calculator and round your answers to 2 decimal places where necessary.

1 $\frac{1}{2}$ **4** $\frac{1}{5}$ **7** $\frac{1}{6}$

2 $\frac{1}{3}$ **5** $\frac{1}{7}$ **8** $\frac{1}{9}$

3 $\frac{1}{4}$ **6** $\frac{1}{8}$ **9** $\frac{1}{10}$

Round these numbers to 2 decimal places.

10 1·124   **13** 2·054   **16** 1·015

11 0·455   **14** 4·781   **17** 6·505

12 7·724   **15** 4·996   **18** 1·078

Write the fraction equivalents of these decimals.

19 0·125   **20** 0·25   **21** 0·1

Write the equivalent decimals for these mixed numbers:

$$1\frac{1}{3} \quad 5\frac{3}{4} \quad 2\frac{2}{5}$$

○ **I am confident with converting fractions to decimals and rounding decimals.**

Multiplying fractions

Complete these fraction multiplications.

1 $\dfrac{1}{2}$ of $\dfrac{1}{5}$

2 $\dfrac{1}{4}$ of $\dfrac{1}{7}$

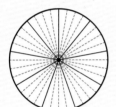

3 $\dfrac{1}{4}$ of $\dfrac{1}{9}$

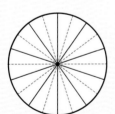

4 $\dfrac{1}{2}$ of $\dfrac{1}{10}$

5 $\dfrac{1}{4} \times \dfrac{1}{6}$

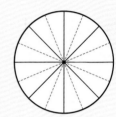

6 $\dfrac{1}{2} \times \dfrac{1}{8}$

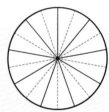

7 $\dfrac{1}{2} \times \dfrac{1}{9}$

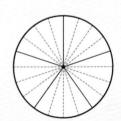

8 $\dfrac{1}{4} \times \dfrac{1}{5}$

Which multiplications have the same answer?
Write two more pairs of questions that have
the same answer as each other.

● I am confident with multiplying fractions that have
○
○ different denominators.

20

Complete these fraction multiplications.

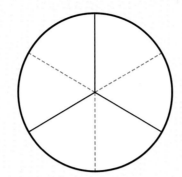

1 $\frac{1}{2} \times \frac{1}{3}$

2 $\frac{1}{4} \times \frac{1}{6}$

3 $\frac{1}{3} \times \frac{1}{7}$

4 $\frac{1}{2} \times \frac{1}{9}$

5 $\frac{1}{4} \times \frac{1}{8}$

6 $\frac{1}{3} \times \frac{1}{6}$

7 $\frac{1}{4} \times \frac{1}{7}$

8 $\frac{1}{3} \times \frac{1}{9}$

9 $\frac{1}{2} \times \frac{1}{8}$

10 $\frac{1}{4} \times \frac{1}{9}$

 Write at least two fraction multiplications with an answer of $\frac{1}{20}$.

○ **I am confident with multiplying fractions that have different denominators.**

Complete these fraction multiplications.

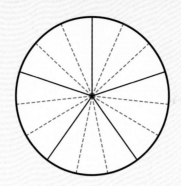

1. $\dfrac{1}{5} \times \dfrac{1}{3}$

2. $\dfrac{1}{8} \times \dfrac{1}{2}$

3. $\dfrac{1}{7} \times \dfrac{1}{4}$

4. $\dfrac{1}{9} \times \dfrac{1}{3}$

5. $\dfrac{1}{5} \times \dfrac{1}{2}$

6. $\dfrac{1}{8} \times \dfrac{1}{3}$

7. $\dfrac{1}{6} \times \dfrac{1}{3}$

8. $\dfrac{1}{8} \times \dfrac{1}{4}$

9. $\dfrac{1}{5} \times \dfrac{1}{4}$

10. $\dfrac{1}{7} \times \dfrac{1}{3}$

 Write at least three fraction multiplications with an answer of $\dfrac{1}{18}$.

I am confident with multiplying fractions that have different denominators.

Complete these fraction multiplications and simplify the answers where necessary.

$$\frac{1}{2} \text{ of } \frac{2}{3}$$

$$\frac{1}{2} \text{ of } \frac{2}{3} = \frac{2}{6} = \frac{1}{3}$$

1 $\frac{1}{2}$ of $\frac{1}{4} = \square$

2 $\frac{1}{5}$ of $\frac{1}{5} = \square$

3 $\frac{1}{3}$ of $\frac{1}{4} = \square$

4 $\frac{1}{4}$ of $\frac{1}{3} = \square$

5 $\frac{1}{2}$ of $\frac{1}{8} = \square$

6 $\frac{1}{3}$ of $\frac{1}{6} = \square$

7 $\frac{1}{4}$ of $\frac{1}{9} = \square$

8 $\frac{1}{5}$ of $\frac{1}{10} = \square$

9 $\frac{1}{5}$ of $\frac{3}{10} = \square$

10 $\frac{1}{4}$ of $\frac{2}{3} = \square$

11 $\frac{1}{5}$ of $\frac{3}{4} = \square$

12 $\frac{1}{3}$ of $\frac{3}{10} = \square$

13 $\frac{1}{2}$ of $\frac{3}{8} = \square$

14 $\frac{1}{4}$ of $\frac{2}{5} = \square$

15 $\frac{1}{5}$ of $\frac{3}{8} = \square$

16 $\frac{1}{4}$ of $\frac{3}{10} = \square$

17 $\frac{1}{3}$ of $\frac{2}{3} = \square$

18 $\frac{1}{3}$ of $\frac{3}{4} = \square$

19 $\frac{1}{5}$ of $\frac{1}{9} = \square$

20 $\frac{1}{4}$ of $\frac{3}{5} = \square$

21 $\frac{1}{2}$ of $\frac{1}{9} = \square$

22 $\frac{1}{3}$ of $\frac{3}{10} = \square$

23 $\frac{1}{3}$ of $\frac{2}{5} = \square$

24 $\frac{1}{4}$ of $\frac{4}{5} = \square$

Write as many fraction multiplications with an answer of $\frac{1}{18}$ as you can.

● ○ ○ **I am confident with multiplying fractions that have different numerators and denominators.**

23

Multiplying decimal numbers

Complete these multiplications.

7 × 4·3

28   2·1

30·1

1 8 × 5·2

40   ☐

☐

2 4 × 3·6

12   ☐

☐

3 (3 × 5·8)

4 (9 × 6·4)

5 (6 × 7·8)

6 (4 × 2·9)

7 (3 × 7·7)

8 (5 × 4·6)

9 (3 × 6·3)

10 (5 × 2·8)

11 (4 × 5·4)

12 (3 × 6·6)

13 (5 × 3·7)

14 (4 × 4·3)

Some children recorded how long it took them to write their name. How long would it take for them to write their name a given number of times?

15 Guy
2·7 seconds
8 times

16 Tracey
5·6 seconds
4 times

17 Catherine
9·2 seconds
7 times

18 Ilesh
6·4 seconds
5 times

19 Elizabeth
9·4 seconds
6 times

20 Davinder
8·7 seconds
3 times

21 Tim
1·9 seconds
7 times

22 Sunam
4·7 seconds
6 times

23 Yasmin
7·3 seconds
4 times

THINK Which children from questions 15 to 23 will be able to write their names more than 8 times in one minute?

○ **I am confident with multiplying 1-place decimal numbers by whole numbers.**

Perform these multiplications using the method shown.

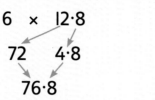

$$6 \times 12{\cdot}8$$
$$72 \quad 4{\cdot}8$$
$$76{\cdot}8$$

1 $5 \times 1{\cdot}3 = \square$

2 $3 \times 2{\cdot}7 = \square$

3 $4 \times 3{\cdot}9 = \square$

4 $3 \times 7{\cdot}6 = \square$

5 $6 \times 4{\cdot}8 = \square$

6 $5 \times 11{\cdot}7 = \square$

7 $4 \times 11{\cdot}6 = \square$

8 $5 \times 12{\cdot}9 = \square$

9 $3 \times 12{\cdot}8 = \square$

10 $4 \times 11{\cdot}5 = \square$

11 $6 \times 12{\cdot}3 = \square$

12 $4 \times 12{\cdot}7 = \square$

 THINK

$$4{\cdot}65 \times 3$$
$$3{\cdot}65 \times 4$$

Explain, without working it out, which of these will give the bigger answer. How do you know?

I am confident with multiplying 1-place decimal numbers by whole numbers.

Perform these multiplications using the methods shown.

 Estimate which of the questions on this page will give the answer closest to 10. Explain why you think this.

4 × 6·7

×	6	0·7
4	24	2·8

= 26·8

If you multiplied your decimal by 10 or 100 to make it easier, remember to divide by the same amount once you have your answer.

① 5 × 1·3 = ☐

② 3 × 2·7 = ☐

③ 4 × 3·9 = ☐

④ 3 × 7·6 = ☐

×	4	0·2	0·04
5	20	1	0·2

= 21·2

⑤ 4 × 0·56 = ☐

⑥ 5 × 1·15 = ☐

⑦ 6 × 1·45 = ☐

⑧ 4 × 2·43 = ☐

Solve these problems.

⑨ Nadia wants to make some curtains. Each curtain is 1·24 m long. She needs to make four pairs of curtains. What length of fabric will she need?

⑩ Maddie is knitting scarves for her six friends. Each scarf is 1·16 m long. How long are the scarves altogether?

I am confident with multiplying 1- and 2-place decimal numbers by whole numbers.

Twelve children each created a decimal multiplication. Whose answer is nearest to 20? Whose is second nearest?

1 Josh 5×4.32

2 Natalie 6×3.78

3 Amit 2×9.41

4 Ben 3×6.75

5 Susie 4×5.23

6 Lucy 7×2.85

7 Narinder 8×2.23

8 Paul 9×1.84

9 Ghopal 4×4.72

10 Katie 7×3.25

11 Poppy 5×4.52

12 Zedekiah 8×8.46

Calculate the perimeters of these regular polygons.

13 a square of side 3·24 cm
14 an octagon of side 5·73 cm
15 a hexagon of side 4·47 cm
16 a hexagon of side 8·67 cm
17 a pentagon of side 7·68 cm

18 a pentagon of side 4·56 cm
19 an equilateral triangle of side 9·28 cm
20 a nonagon of side 6·83 cm
21 an octagon of side 6·84 cm

| 2 | 3 | 7 |

Arrange these digits to make a decimal number between 1 and 10 that will give an answer close to 26 when multiplied by 8.

27

Choose three of the four digits to make the multiplication correct.

1

2	3
4	7

$\square.\square\square$
$\times \quad\quad\quad 6$
_____
$28 \cdot 32$

4

7	8
6	9

$\square.\square\square$
$\times \quad\quad\quad 8$
_____
$55 \cdot 12$

2

3	4
6	8

$\square.\square\square$
$\times \quad\quad\quad 5$
_____
$19 \cdot 20$

5

4	7
6	5

$\square.\square\square$
$\times \quad\quad\quad 9$
_____
$51 \cdot 84$

3

4	2
5	3

$\square.\square\square$
$\times \quad\quad\quad 7$
_____
$30 \cdot 24$

6

5	7
6	8

$\square.\square\square$
$\times \quad\quad\quad 4$
_____
$30 \cdot 32$

Solve these problems.

7 Jim has 8 pieces of fencing, each 1·86 cm long. He needs to build a fence 20 m long. How long would his fence be at the moment, and how many more pieces of fencing does he need to buy?

8 Kate and 6 of her friends are going on a train journey. The tickets cost £6·38 each. How much change will they have from £50?

 THINK
$3 \cdot 27 \times 4 = 6 \cdot 54 \times 2$
Can you find other pairs like this that have the same answer?

I am confident with multiplying 2-place decimal numbers by whole numbers.

These items are for sale in a clothes shop.

£6·75
£5·45
£11·43
£13·23
£21·96
£28·76
£14·67

Calculate how much it would cost to buy the following items.

1. Six t-shirts
2. Four pairs of trousers
3. Seven jumpers
4. Five t-shirts
5. Eight pairs of shorts
6. Seven pairs of trousers

7. Three hats
8. Nine dresses
9. Seven pairs of shorts
10. Six jumpers
11. Three pairs of trainers
12. Eight hats

 Use the digits 2 and 4 to create the largest amount possible.

£ ☐ ☐ · ☐ ☐ × ☐

 I am confident with multiplying 2-place decimal money amounts by whole numbers.

Multiplying 3- and 4-digit numbers

367 × 26

×	300	60	7
20	6000	1200	140
6	1800	360	42

```
    6 0 0 0
    1 2 0 0
    1 8 0 0
      3 6 0
      1 4 0
+      4 2
   ‾‾‾‾‾‾‾
    1 1
   ‾‾‾‾‾‾‾
    9 5 4 2
```

You can write the addition as column addition. You could still add some parts in your head to make your column addition shorter.

1 434 × 27

×	400	30	4
20			
7			

2 586 × 26

×	500	80	6
20			
6			

3 967 × 24

×	900	60	7
20			
4			

4 849 × 23

×	800	40	9
20			
3			

5 4231 × 23

×	4000	200	30	1
20				
3				

6 5484 × 26

×	5000	400	80	4
20				
6				

7 3657 × 28

×	3000	600	50	7
20				
8				

8 9578 × 27

×	9000	500	70	8
20				
7				

THINK What are the missing numbers in this multiplication?

×	?	?	?
?	8000	1400	60
?	3200	560	24

● I am confident with multiplying 3- and 4-digit numbers
○ using the grid method.
○

Perform these multiplications.

1 482
    × 16
    ____

2 567
    × 23
    ____

3 346
    × 27
    ____

4 907
    × 29
    ____

```
    5 4 1 6
  ×     1 5
  _____
  5 4 1 6 0
  2 7²0 8³0
    1   1
  _____
  8 1 2 4 0
```

When we multiply by 10 we move the digits one place to the left. Here we multiplied by 10, then by 5, then added the answers together.

You can use place value, adding and short multiplication to help you.

5 3627
    ×   13
    ____

6 2446
    ×   14
    ____

7 5624
    ×   26
    ____

8 7894
    ×   24
    ____

 Look at this multiplication. Work out what digit each letter represents.

```
      A B C D
    ×     1 6
    _____
    4 4 5 3 0
    2 6²7³1¹8
```

I am confident with multiplying 3- and 4-digit numbers by 2-digit numbers.

Work out the answers to these multiplications.

1   7486
  ×   23
  ‾‾‾‾‾‾

2   6738
  ×   24
  ‾‾‾‾‾‾

3   4547
  ×   27
  ‾‾‾‾‾‾

4   6748
  ×   28
  ‾‾‾‾‾‾

5   6686
  ×   26
  ‾‾‾‾‾‾

6   4783
  ×   29
  ‾‾‾‾‾‾

7   5685
  ×   31
  ‾‾‾‾‾‾

8   5693
  ×   32
  ‾‾‾‾‾‾

Solve these problems.

9   How many hours are there in 2647 days?

10 A factory makes boxes of chocolates.
    There are 32 chocolates in each box. How
    many chocolates are there in 3756 boxes?

11 Jasper uses a cycling app. It tells him that he has been
    on 1632 rides and that he rides, on average, 28 km each
    time. What is the total distance he has ridden?

12 Tom plays a skateboarding game on his games console.
    He scores 5423 points for each trick and does 37 tricks.
    How many points has he scored?

●
● ⠀**I am confident with multiplying 4-digit numbers by**
● ⠀**2-digit numbers.**

Use the grid method to solve these multiplication problems.

1 It costs £356 for one person to fly to Spain. How much would it cost for 16 people?

2 Lucy paid £482 to fly to Morocco. How much would it have cost for 24 people?

3 Beth paid £598 to fly to South Africa. How much would it have cost for 17 people?

4 Urvi paid £177 to fly to Prague. How much would it have cost for 23 people?

5 Dinesh paid £386 to fly to India. How much would it have cost for 28 people?

6 Greg paid £773 to fly to China. How much would it have cost for 19 people?

7 Amanda paid £552 to fly to Dubai. How much would it have cost for 25 people?

8 Deepa paid £694 to fly to New York. How much would it have cost for 27 people?

9 Connor paid £1342 to fly to New Zealand. How much would it have cost for 16 people?

10 Theo paid £4421 for an 'around the world' ticket. How much would it have cost for 23 tickets?

 15 people fly to Tenerife. They want to spend less than £9500. What is the most their flight can cost per person?

● I am confident with multiplying 3- and 4-digit money amounts by 2-digit numbers.

Copy each quadrilateral onto square dotted paper.
Write its name and draw the diagonals.

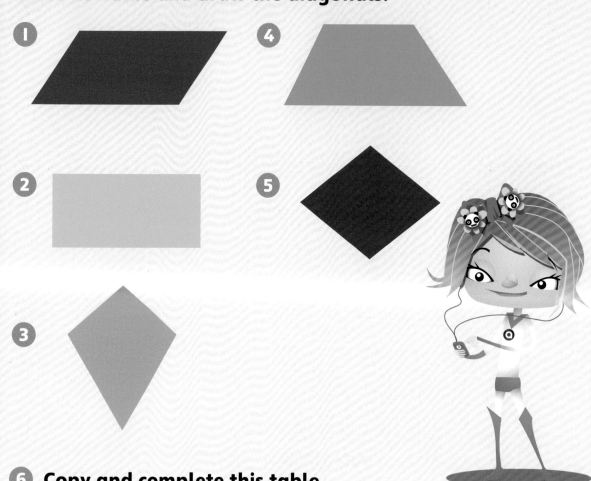

1

4

2

5

3

6 **Copy and complete this table.**

Shape	Diagonals bisect?	Bisect at 90°?
Parallelogram		✗
Rectangle	✔	Sometimes
Kite		
Trapezium		
Rhombus		
Square		

I am confident with identifying properties of
quadrilaterals.

Work out the missing angles in these quadrilaterals.

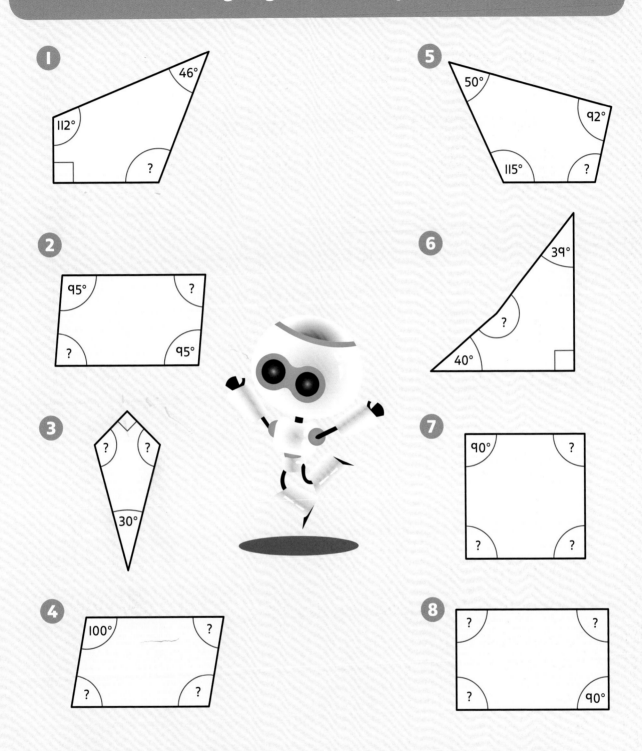

1. 46° 112° ?

5. 50° 92° 115° ?

2. 95° ? ? 95°

6. 39° ? 40°

3. ? ? 30°

7. 90° ? ? ?

4. 100° ? ? ?

8. ? ? ? 90°

THINK Is it possible to draw a quadrilateral with three angles of more than 90°? Is it possible to draw a quadrilateral with an angle of more than 180°?

 I am confident with identifying missing angles in quadrilaterals.

Work out the missing angles in these quadrilaterals and triangles.

1

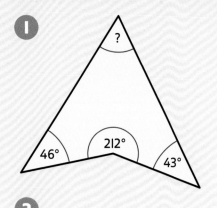

2

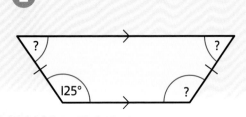

3

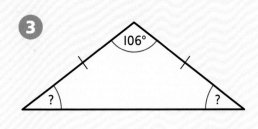

4

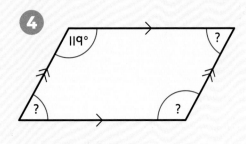

5

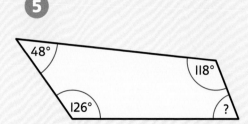

6

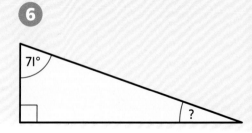

7

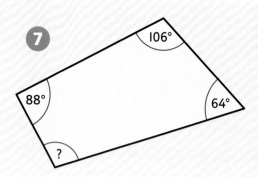

8

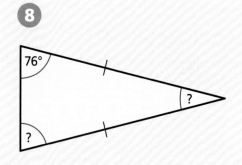

 Draw an irregular quadrilateral with one acute, one obtuse and one reflex angle.

Work out the missing angles in these triangles, quadrilaterals and hexagons.

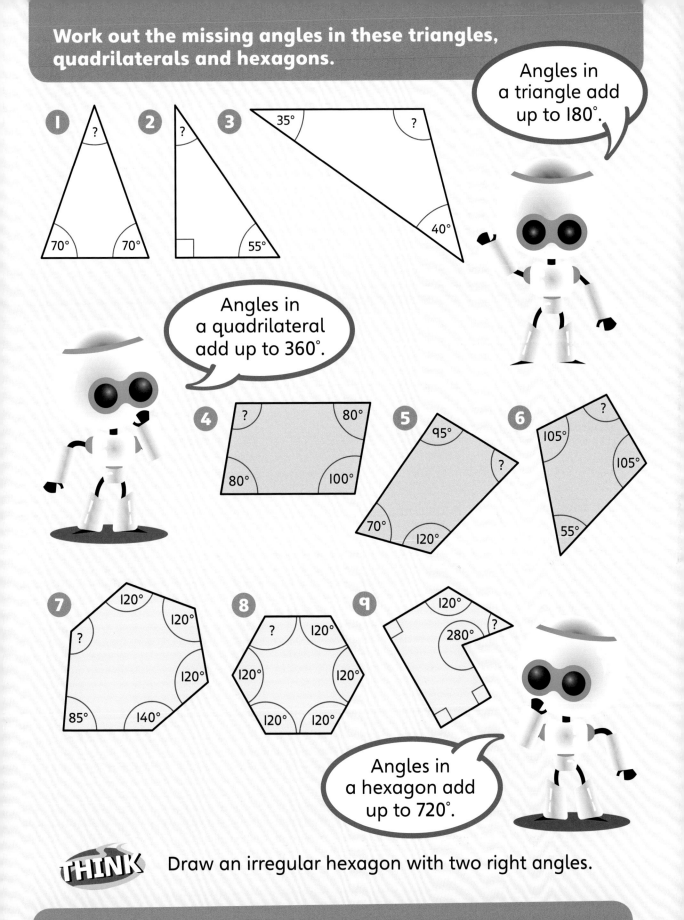

Angles in a triangle add up to 180°.

① ? / 70° / 70°

② ? / 55°

③ 35° / ? / 40°

Angles in a quadrilateral add up to 360°.

④ ? / 80° / 80° / 100°

⑤ 95° / ? / 70° / 120°

⑥ ? / 105° / 105° / 55°

⑦ 120° / 120° / ? / 120° / 85° / 140°

⑧ ? / 120° / 120° / 120° / 120° / 120°

⑨ 120° / ? / 280°

Angles in a hexagon add up to 720°.

THINK   Draw an irregular hexagon with two right angles.

○ I am confident with identifying missing angles
○ in quadrilaterals, triangles and hexagons.

37

Work out the missing angles in these hexagons and pentagons.

1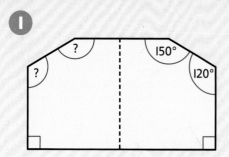

2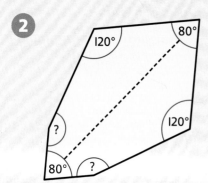

3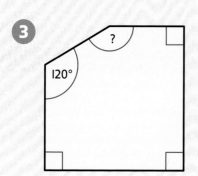

4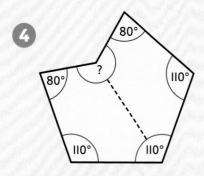

5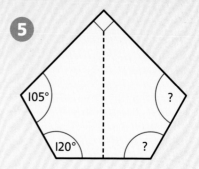

6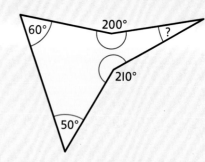

7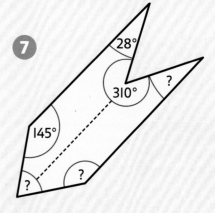

 Draw an irregular hexagon with two reflex angles. Can you draw one with three?

I am confident with identifying missing angles in pentagons and hexagons.

Measure these circles carefully and answer the questions.

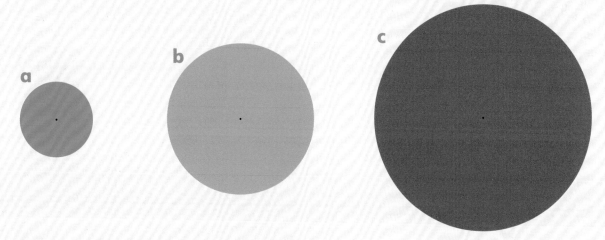

a

b

c

1. Measure the radius of circle a.

2. Measure the diameter of circle b.

3. Measure the radius of circle c.

4. **Draw these circles.**

3 cm

2 cm

4 cm

○ **I am confident with measuring and drawing circles.**

Write the names of these parts of a circle.

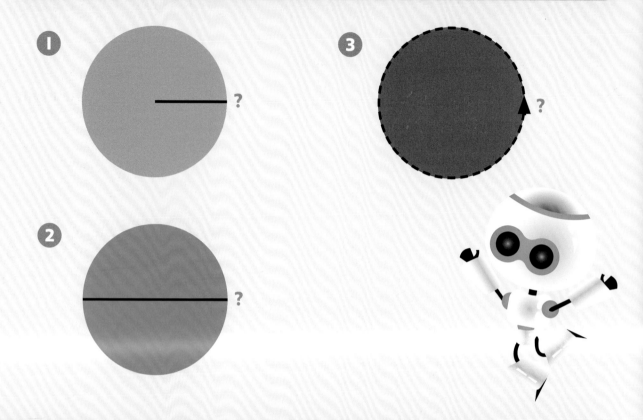

1. ?

2. ?

3. ?

Use a pair of compasses to draw circles with:

4. a radius of 3 cm

5. a radius of 6 cm

6. a radius of 9·5 cm

7. a diameter of 11 cm

8. a diameter of 17 cm

9. a radius of 5·5 cm

10. a diameter of 16 cm

11. a diameter of 14·5 cm.

 Use one of your circles. Think of a way of measuring the circumference. Is there a relation between the circumference and the diameter?

I am confident with measuring and drawing circles.

40

Use a ruler and a protractor to draw these shapes. Label all of the angles and sides and work out any missing ones.

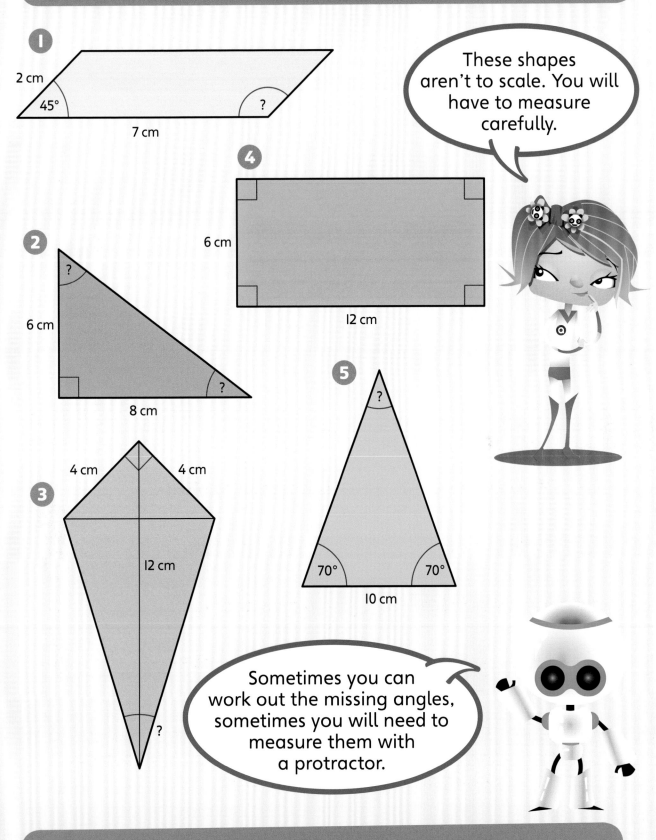

These shapes aren't to scale. You will have to measure carefully.

1
2 cm
45°
7 cm
?

4
6 cm
12 cm

2
?
6 cm
8 cm
?

5
?
70°   70°
10 cm

3
4 cm   4 cm
12 cm
?

Sometimes you can work out the missing angles, sometimes you will need to measure them with a protractor.

Adding using mental methods

Choose a method to complete these additions.

1 $3407 + 23\,050 = \square$

2 $45\,251 + 2104 = \square$

3 $34 + 62 = \square$

4 $426 + 299 = \square$

5 $3{\cdot}4 + 24{\cdot}6 = \square$

6 $4{\cdot}7 + 23{\cdot}3 = \square$

7 $4632 + 31\,230 = \square$

8 $3406 + 2344 = \square$

9 $73 + 26 = \square$

10 $352 + 201 = \square$

11 $52{\cdot}3 + 6{\cdot}7 = \square$

12 $546 + 101 = \square$

13 $7917 + 2072 = \square$

14 $60 + 120 + 40 = \square$

15 $42\,161 + 9999 = \square$

16 $14{\cdot}6 + 15{\cdot}4 = \square$

17 $999 + 999 = \square$

18 $62 + 62 = \square$

THINK

$7{\cdot}3 + 3{\cdot}7 = 11$
Write some more pairs of 1-place decimal numbers between 1 and 10 which are the reverse of each other and also add to 11.

○
○ **I am confident with adding numbers using different**
○ **mental methods.**

THINK Look at these additions. Write the numbers of the questions you are going to answer using rounding. Then list those you will answer using place-value calculations.

Now complete the additions using your chosen methods.

18·36 + 9·9

Chosen method is rounding:

18·36 + 10 − 0·1 = 28·36
28·36 − 0·1 = 28·26

It will be easier to use place-value calculations to solve some of these questions, and rounding for others.

1 13·08 + 5·9 = ☐

7 68·37 + 0·509 = ☐

2 5 152 357 + 33 500 = ☐

8 103 204 + 26 740 = ☐

3 8500·5 + 487 = ☐

9 13·99 + 6·08 = ☐

4 4·76 + 7·99 = ☐

10 64 003 + 2950 = ☐

5 15·146 + 6·7 = ☐

11 36·9 + 12·7 = ☐

6 8·3 + 6·6 + 5·7 = ☐

12 57 000 + 26 000 = ☐

I am confident with adding using place value, rounding and number facts.

Adding using the column method

Perform these additions.

① 583 973
+   75 895

② 859 364
+   22 785

③   45 583
+   3 609

④ 957 736
+ 559 809

⑤ 3 685 142
+   826 864

⑥ 716 349
+ 589 932

⑦ 3 563 826
+   856 679

⑧ 8 882 578
+ 3 241 894

⑨ 9 133 628
   5 674 956
+   949 838

 **THINK**   Write an addition like this where the answer is a 7-digit number with as many zeros as possible.

⦿ **I am confident with adding 2 or 3 numbers using the**
○
○ **column method.**

Subtracting using mental methods

Choose a mental method to complete these subtractions.

1
```
  17 329
-  6 009
```

2
```
  47 894
-  1 802
```

3
```
  382 483
-  10 402
```

4
```
  573 568
- 140 008
```

5 32 846 – 1999 = ☐

6 27·6 – 4·99 = ☐

7 46·5 – 9·99 = ☐

8 242 – 199 = ☐

9 73 – 48 = ☐

10 218 – 194 = ☐

11 312 – 257 = ☐

12 92 – 67 = ☐

THINK Write a subtraction to match this:
```
  ABC
- CBA
```

where B = 0 and the difference between A and C is always 2. Try it several times. Do you always get the same answer?

○ **I am confident with subtracting using the mental**
○ **methods of place value, rounding and counting up.**
○

Subtracting using the column method

Perform these subtractions.

①
```
   96 978
 - 84 891
 _____
```

⑥
```
   716 361
 - 581 932
 _____
```

②
```
   69 964
 - 23 285
 _____
```

⑦
```
   3 767 088
 -   453 636
 _____
```

③
```
   57 718
 - 49 824
 _____
```

⑧
```
   5 738 158
 -   574 956
 _____
```

④
```
   285 683
 - 163 609
 _____
```

⑨
```
   8 862 579
 - 3 241 494
 _____
```

⑤
```
   619 179
 - 376 864
 _____
```

⑩
```
   6 308 574
 - 3 143 331
 _____
```

 **THINK** Choose two of your subtractions and check them using addition.

○ **I am confident with subtracting 5-, 6- and 7-digit numbers.**

1   471 819
      − 163 667

2   679 124
      − 314 391

3   546 178
      − 376 864

4   723 717
      − 351 824

5   619 153
      − 473 285

6   824 352
      − 286 465

7   6 796 574
      − 3 581 932

8   6 716 861
      − 3 143 337

9   9 738 138
      − 2 571 453

10 7 147 029
      − 5 453 636

Use Frog to solve 100 000 − 9987.
Now solve 99 999 − 9987 using
column subtraction. Compare your
answers. What do you notice?

Choosing methods for addition and subtraction

Solve these word problems.

1 At a football ground there are 75 811 seats. If 1301 of them are empty, how many seats are being used?

2 An international Stadium has 90 000 seats. How many empty seats are there if 79 989 are being used?

3 A forklift truck picks up two crates. One weighs 48 673 g and the other weighs 49 999 g. What is the total weight of the two crates?

4 Mr Jones worked out that he was 15 583 days old. He worked out that his wife was 1413 days older than him. How many days old was his wife?

5 A famous footballer earns £11 475 274 in one year. In the following year he earns £738 185 more. How much does he earn in the second year?

6 A company makes plastic ducks. In January 45 618 ducks are made. In February there is a problem with one of the machines and 15 785 fewer ducks than in January are made. How many ducks are made in both January and February altogether?

○ **I am confident with solving addition and subtraction**
○
○ **word problems.**

Solve these word problems.

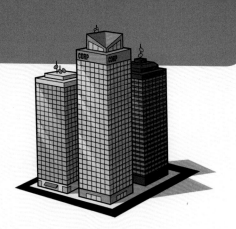

1 A skyscraper has 26 568 windows. In one month a team of window cleaners clean 15 365 of them. How many windows still need to be cleaned?

2 The distance from the Earth to the Moon is 384 400 km. The distance from the Earth to Venus, when it is at its closest to Earth, is 38 000 000 km. What is the difference between these two distances?

3 A blue whale weighs 2700 kg at birth. By the time it is an adult it has gained an extra 184 735 kg. What is the weight of the adult blue whale?

4 A famous popstar earns £12 288 945 in one year. In the following year she earns £463 286 more. How much does she earn in the two years altogether?

5 A large company made profits of £4 582 421 in 2012. In 2013 their profits were £29 999 less than in 2012. What were their total profits for the two years altogether?

6 A scientist measures 4·62 ml of acid into a test tube. With a pipette she carefully takes out 0·015 ml of the acid. Finally, she adds 1·205 ml of water into the test tube. How much liquid is in the test tube now?

○ **I am confident with solving addition and subtraction**
○ **word problems.**
○

Identifying factors and multiples

Look at a multiplication grid and write all the numbers that are multiples of these numbers.

1 7 **3** 9

2 4

Write the numbers that are common multiples of these pairs.

4 2 and 3 **7** 4 and 6

5 3 and 4 **8** 4 and 8

6 2 and 7 **9** 4 and 5

Write the smallest common multiples of the following pairs.

10 2 and 3 **14** 2 and 4 **18** 6 and 8

11 2 and 5 **15** 3 and 12 **19** 8 and 10

12 3 and 4 **16** 4 and 6 **20** 10 and 15

13 3 and 5 **17** 8 and 12 **21** 25 and 30

THINK 12 is a common multiple of 2, 3 and 4. Work out another number that is a common multiple of consecutive numbers.

● **I am confident with working out and identifying**
○
○ **multiples of 1- and 2-digit numbers.**
○

Write three common multiples for each set of numbers.

1 **2** **7**

2 **3** **4**

3 **5** **3**

4 **6** **10**

5 **4** **5**

6 **5** **15**

7 **25** **20**

8 **4** **9**

9 **5** **8**

10 **2** **6** **5**

11 **3** **4** **5**

12 **10** **15** **25**

Use one set of 2–9 number cards.
Investigate all of the different possible pairs
of cards and the smallest common multiple
of each pair. You can record them in a table.

×	2	3	4
2	4	6	8
3			
4			

How many different common multiples are there?

I am confident with working out and identifying
multiples of 1- and 2-digit numbers.

51

Identifying prime numbers

1 On squared paper, copy and continue this number spiral up to 80. Colour the prime numbers. Describe any patterns they make.

		3	4	5
	11	2	1	6
	10	9	8	7

I am a prime number. Who am I?

2 I am between 20 and 70. My digits total 10.

5 I am the fourth prime number after 40.

3 I am a 2-digit number. My digits have a difference of 7.

6 I am between 25 and 42. My units digit is a prime number.

4 I am the third prime number after 20.

7 I am between 40 and 80. When my digits are reversed I am another prime number.

8 Use one set of 1–9 number cards to make prime numbers.

Make four prime numbers using six cards.　　　31 47　2 5
Make four prime numbers using seven cards.　　61 29　47 3

Can you use more than seven cards to make a prime number?

 THINK 17 and 71 are both prime numbers. Find other pairs of reversed numbers where both are prime numbers.

- I am confident with identifying prime numbers and number patterns.

Decide if these statements are true or false.

1. All prime numbers are odd numbers.
2. There are ten prime numbers less than 30.
3. All prime numbers have exactly two factors.
4. The total of two prime numbers is always an even number.
5. Every number next to a multiple of 6 is a prime number.
6. Every 2-digit prime number is next to a multiple of 6.
7. Every 2-digit multiple of 6 is next to a prime number.
8. There is only one 2-digit prime number that has 6 as a tens digit.
9. 1 is not a prime number.
10. All 2-digit prime numbers have a ones digit of 1, 3, 7 or 9.
11. There are four prime numbers between 10 and 20.
12. A square number cannot be a prime number.

Solve this problem.

13. These pairs of prime numbers have a total of 90

7 and 83   11 and 79

Can you find seven more pairs like this?

THINK Large prime numbers are used as security codes because they are difficult to crack. Find some prime numbers greater than 100. Try to find some very large ones. Use a divisibility test to help you.

I am confident with identifying prime numbers.

DIVISION INVESTIGATION

Perform these divisions. Many of them have a remainder.

1. 1111 ÷ 5 = ☐

2. 2222 ÷ 5 = ☐

3. 3333 ÷ 5 = ☐

4. 4444 ÷ 5 = ☐

5. 5555 ÷ 5 = ☐

6. 6666 ÷ 5 = ☐

7. 7777 ÷ 5 = ☐

8. 8888 ÷ 5 = ☐

9. 9999 ÷ 5 = ☐

10. Then divide the same numbers by 6.

11. What do you notice about the remainder in each case?

What happens if you divide the same numbers:

12. by 7?

13. by 3?

14. by 8?

15. by 9?

● I am confident with using short division to divide
4-digit numbers by 1-digit numbers.

Long division

Perform these divisions, giving any remainder as a fraction.

Look at the divisor and write its times-table up to 10 to help you solve your division.

$$12 \overline{)496}$$

$$
\begin{array}{r}
40 + 1 + \frac{4}{12} \\
12 \overline{)496} \\
-480 \\
\hline
16 \\
12 \\
\hline
4
\end{array}
$$

12
24
36
48
60
72
84
96
108
120

Begin by seeing how many lots of the divisor will fit into the number.

1 $12 \overline{)625}$

2 $12 \overline{)758}$

3 $25 \overline{)578}$

4 $13 \overline{)418}$

5 $13 \overline{)557}$

6 $25 \overline{)789}$

7 $13 \overline{)678}$

8 $25 \overline{)879}$

9 $25 \overline{)301}$

 THINK Choose two of your divisions. Check your answers using multiplication.

○ **I am confident with using long division to divide**
○
○ **3-digit numbers by 2-digit numbers.**

Use long division to perform these calculations.
Write any remainders as fractions.

 Estimate which division will have the biggest answer.

> Look at the divisor and write its times-table up to 10 to help you solve your division.

1   13 | 566

5   13 | 749

9   13 | 793

2   25 | 903

6   14 | 473

10   25 | 269

3   14 | 497

7   21 | 789

11   14 | 895

4   21 | 912

8   25 | 896

12   21 | 397

 Choose two divisions. Check your answers using multiplication.

● I am confident with using long division to divide 3-digit
  numbers by 2-digit numbers.

Use long division to perform these calculations. Write any remainders as fractions.

Use your times tables' knowledge to help you.

1 16 $\overline{)754}$

2 32 $\overline{)267}$

3 25 $\overline{)953}$

4 24 $\overline{)798}$

5 32 $\overline{)783}$

6 25 $\overline{)482}$

7 24 $\overline{)806}$

8 16 $\overline{)739}$

9 25 $\overline{)695}$

10 16 $\overline{)888}$

11 24 $\overline{)785}$

12 32 $\overline{)794}$

Divide 992 by 32. Divide 992 by 16. What do you notice about the answers? Find a quick way to divide 1344 by 16 and by 32.

Practise long division by performing these calculations. Write any remainders as fractions.

1 14 | 182

5 14 | 789

9 25 | 860

2 14 | 728

6 14 | 999

10 25 | 777

3 14 | 337

7 25 | 325

11 25 | 745

4 14 | 450

8 25 | 626

12 25 | 433

Divide 384 by 24 using long division. Then divide 384 by 12 using short division. Compare the answers. Can you use what you discover to find an easy way to divide 432 by 24?

● **I am confident with using long division to divide 3-digit**
numbers by 2-digit numbers.

Practise long division by performing these calculations. Write any remainders as fractions.

① 14 ⟌ 1862

② 15 ⟌ 3728

③ 16 ⟌ 3456

④ 23 ⟌ 4560

⑤ 24 ⟌ 4675

⑥ 23 ⟌ 7489

⑦ 16 ⟌ 9969

⑧ 15 ⟌ 6325

⑨ 24 ⟌ 6726

⑩ 14 ⟌ 3284

⑪ 15 ⟌ 8675

⑫ 24 ⟌ 7777

⑬ 23 ⟌ 7843

⑭ 14 ⟌ 5826

⑮ 16 ⟌ 5739

Divide 5616 by 24 using long division. Then divide 5616 by 12 using short division. Compare the answers. Can you use what you discover to find an easy way to divide 5832 by 24?

● I am confident with using long division to divide 4-digit
○ numbers by 2-digit numbers.
○

Calculating change

£4·85

£19·87

£81·59

£78·42

£53·17

£63·70

£28·63

You have £150 to spend in this skate shop. Work out the change you would get if you bought these items.

1 the skateboard and the wheels

2 the scooter and the helmet

3 the rollerblades and the knee pads

4 the ramp and the skateboard

5 the helmet and the knee pads

6 the scooter and the rollerblades

Solve this problem.

7 Sam buys two items. One costs £23·48. He gets the same amount of change from £100 as the second item costs. How much is the second item?

○ **I am confident with calculating change.**
○
○

Calculate the change.

You have £200 to spend on spy-gear. Work out the change you would get if you bought these items.

1. the night-vision goggles and the disguise
2. the binoculars and the zip wire
3. the invisible ink and the code book
4. the zip wire, the code book and the invisible ink
5. the binoculars, the night-vision goggles and the disguise
6. the invisible ink, the binoculars and the code book
7. the night-vision goggles, the code book and the zip wire

 Kim buys two items: £AB·BC and £CB·BA. The change from £200 is £14·43. Work out what digits are represented by A, B and C.

○ **I am confident with calculating change.**
○
○

Adding and subtracting decimal numbers

Perform these decimal subtractions.

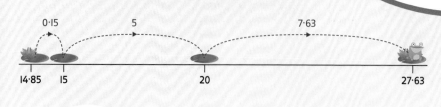

27·63 – 14·85 = 12·78

Remember to jump to the next whole number, then the next multiple of 10, then on to the final number.

0·15   5   7·63

14·85   15   20   27·63

Try not to confuse decimal jumps and whole numbers.

1 38·43 – 27·82 = ☐

2 26·55 – 18·73 = ☐

3 35·27 – 26·13 = ☐

4 43·49 – 37·77 = ☐

5 59·58 – 46·05 = ☐

6 63·32 – 54·88 = ☐

7 65·72 – 48·69 = ☐

8 72·08 – 66·45 = ☐

9 84·35 – 71·63 = ☐

10 50·94 – 38·17 = ☐

11 75·49 – 69·36 = ☐

12 94·01 – 79·26 = ☐

THINK Draw a Frog subtraction that involves three jumps and ends on 30. The first jump should be a 2-place decimal and the second jump is less than 10.

I am confident with performing subtractions of 2-place decimal numbers.

Complete these calculations using mental methods.

1 $16·8 + 4·12 = \boxed{}$

3 $24·63 - 8·2 = \boxed{}$

2 $30·54 + 7·41 = \boxed{}$

4 $36·58 - 4·35 = \boxed{}$

Use column addition to perform these calculations.

5
$$\begin{array}{r} 45·76 \\ + \ 18·21 \\ \hline \end{array}$$

7
$$\begin{array}{r} 34·28 \\ + \ 17·37 \\ \hline \end{array}$$

6
$$\begin{array}{r} 54·84 \\ + \ 41·62 \\ \hline \end{array}$$

8
$$\begin{array}{r} 37·57 \\ + \ 25·62 \\ \hline \end{array}$$

Use Frog to perform these subtractions.

9 $7·42 - 3·86 = \boxed{}$

11 $12·67 - 9·73 = \boxed{}$

10 $11·33 - 4·79 = \boxed{}$

12 $24·52 - 18·69 = \boxed{}$

 Cat has used Frog to solve a subtraction but she thinks she has got the wrong answer! Help her by finding her mistake and then showing her how to solve it correctly.

2·2   3   0·4

1·78   2   5   5·4

$5·4 - 1·78 = 5·6$

○ **I am confident with using different methods to solve**
○ **decimal additions and subtractions.**

Choose a method to perform these calculations.

> You could use mental or column methods to perform these.

1 3·14 + 8·72 = ☐

2 14·86 + 35·48 + 12·57 = ☐

3 23·18 − 15·04 = ☐

4 14·7 − 3·2 = ☐

5 62·63 − 57·94 = ☐

6 54·36 + 15·69 = ☐

7 12·3 + 4·02 = ☐

8 37·46 − 14·01 = ☐

9 36·83 + 8·78 = ☐

10 47·48 − 10·16 = ☐

11 53·24 + 28·32 + 9·45 = ☐

12 47·02 − 39·98 = ☐

THINK Cat has used Frog to solve a subtraction but she thinks she has got the wrong answer! Help her by finding any mistakes and then showing her how to solve it correctly.

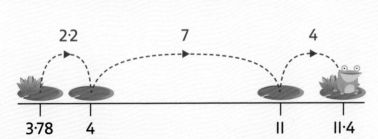

2·2   7   4

3·78   4   11   11·4

11·4 − 3·78 = 9·6

● I am confident with choosing different methods to solve decimal additions and subtractions.

Perform these decimal additions to help Sarah.

1 Sarah has some clues to the code of the lock of the cupboard her computer games are kept in. She knows the combination is two of these numbers added together but she is not sure which two.

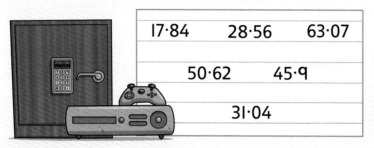

17·84	28·56	63·07
50·62	45·9	
31·04		

Add together six different pairs of numbers to show Sarah different methods she could use to get into the cupboard. Why is it a good idea to use different methods for different pairs?

Complete these calculations and say which method you used.

2 85·73 – 78·68 = ☐

3 14·02 – 7·4 = ☐

4 85·03 – 79·99 = ☐

5 34·83 – 29·61 = ☐

Decide if each of these statements is true or false. Can you explain how you know?

6 Subtracting a number ending in ·55 from a 2-place decimal number always gives an odd number of hundredths.

7 Adding two 2-place decimal numbers never gives a 1-place decimal total.

8 Subtracting a 2-place decimal number from 100 always gives a 2-place decimal number answer.

9 Subtracting a 2-place decimal number from its reversed number, for example 86·61 – 16·68, always gives an answer where the digits add to a multiple of 9.

○ **I am confident with using different methods to solve decimal additions and subtractions.**

Solve these word problems.

1 Alicia has decided to wallpaper her rectangular attic. She needs to find the perimeter so she knows how much paper to buy. The length is 5·27 m and the width is 3·86 m. What is the perimeter?

2 Rani is a painter and decorator. In one week, she uses 11·94 l of white paint and 7·7 l of magnolia paint. How much more white paint does she use than magnolia?

3 In a diving competition, Theo receives scores of 9·2, 8·9 and 8·8 points. What is his total score?

4 Usain Bolt ran 100 m in 9·58 seconds. The fastest under-18 sprinter ran 100 m in 10·19 seconds. How much faster was Usain Bolt?

5 A bushel is an imperial measure. One bushel of barley weighs 21·77 kg. Mr Archer had a sack of barley containing 2 bushels but he took out 13·5 kg from it. What is the weight of the barley in the sack now?

6 Charlie has £57·68 in her wallet and £59·57 in her bank account. She uses her money to buy a computer game that costs £112·46. How much money does she have now?

7 A chain is another imperial measure. Railway workers sometimes still use chains to measure distances. One chain is 20·12 m. A piece of track that needs repairing is 14·5 m less than 6 chains past the station. How far away is it in metres?

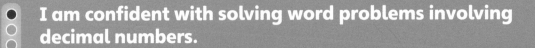

○ **I am confident with solving word problems involving**
○ **decimal numbers.**

Solve these word problems.

1. Matilda went on a cycling holiday. She rode 74·82 miles on the first day. On the second day she rode 65·73 miles. She wants to cover 200 miles in three days. How far does she need to ride on the third day?

2. Simon is a chocolatier. In one week, he uses 5·36 kg of white chocolate. He uses 8·28 kg more dark chocolate than white chocolate. If the white and dark chocolate each cost £2 per kilogram, how much did Simon spend on chocolate that week?

3. A scientist measures 4·62 ml of a chemical into a beaker. With a pipette, he carefully takes out 0·67 ml of the chemical. Finally, he adds 1·25 ml of water into the beaker. How much liquid is in the beaker now?

4. The women's 400 m world record is 47·60 seconds. The 16th fastest women's 400 m runner ran it in 49·24 seconds. What time is exactly halfway between these two times?

5. Each gold and silver medal from an athletics competition weighed 0·41 kg. The bronze medal weighed 0·05 kg less. What was the total weight of the medals held by a person who won one gold, one silver and two bronze medals?

6. Amy has £54·68 in her wallet, £32·45 in her piggy bank and £42·58 in her bank account. How much more does she need to save to reach £200?

THINK · Each letter stands for a digit. No two different letters represent the same digit. Work out what each letter stands for.

$$
\begin{array}{r}
\text{S·NOW} \\
+\ \text{R·AIN} \\
\hline
\text{SL·EET}
\end{array}
$$

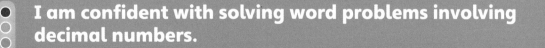

Calculating averages

Each player in a team took 10 penalties. These are the numbers of goals scored. Calculate the mean number of goals scored by the players in each team.

Reds: 5 + 7 + 4 + 7 + 7 = ☐

☐ ÷ 5 = ☐

1. Reds: 5, 7, 4, 7, 7

2. Yellows: 8, 2, 7, 4, 4

3. Maroons: 3, 2, 5, 4, 4, 6

4. Greys: 8, 7, 7, 6

5. Whites: 6, 10, 8, 9, 9, 9, 5

6. Greens: 4, 3, 6, 5, 5, 7

7. Stripes: 6, 6, 8, 7, 9, 6

8. Now write the teams in order based on their mean scores, starting with the highest score.

9. For each team, write the range of goals scored.

THINK Write a set of 10 goal scores for a team where the mean is 7.

○ **I am confident with calculating mean averages.**
○
○

These are the temperatures in °C found in different cities at the start of December. Find the mean temperature for each city.

1 London 7, 7, 6, 5, 5, 7, 8, 7, 7, 6

2 Edinburgh 8, 8, 6, 6, 4, 5, 6, 7, 6, 6, 4

3 Athens 18, 18, 20, 20, 19, 18, 17, 19, 21, 21, 17, 20

4 Paris 9, 10, 12, 10, 11, 13, 12, 10, 9, 11, 10, 8, 11, 9, 5

5 Dublin 6, 6, 7, 4, 6, 7, 6, 9, 6, 8, 6, 7, 5, 8

6 Cairo 24, 25, 21, 24, 22, 20, 23, 21

7 Sydney 38, 36, 35, 36, 34, 33, 35, 33, 33, 32

8 Singapore 28, 28, 27, 28, 28, 27, 25, 26, 29, 28, 29, 27

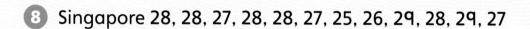

● **I am confident with calculating mean averages.**
○
○

Reading line graphs

Use a ruler to help you read from the line graph.

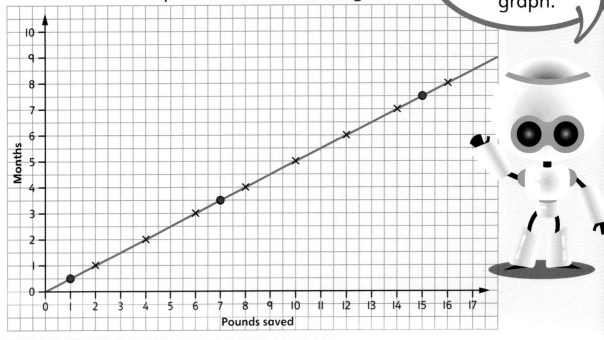

Graph to show Sunil's savings

How much has Sunil saved after:

1 2 months?   3 4 months?   5 $4\frac{1}{2}$ months? 7 $5\frac{1}{2}$ months?

2 3 months?   4 8 months?   6 $2\frac{1}{2}$ months? 8 $6\frac{1}{2}$ months?

How long has Sunil been saving when he has:

9 £4?   11 £2?   13 £13?

10 £12?   12 £5?

14 Look at the red points. Write what each point tells you.

THINK   How much had Sunil saved after 9 weeks?
How much had he saved after 15 weeks?

● I am confident with reading and interpreting line graphs.

Look at this graph and answer the questions.

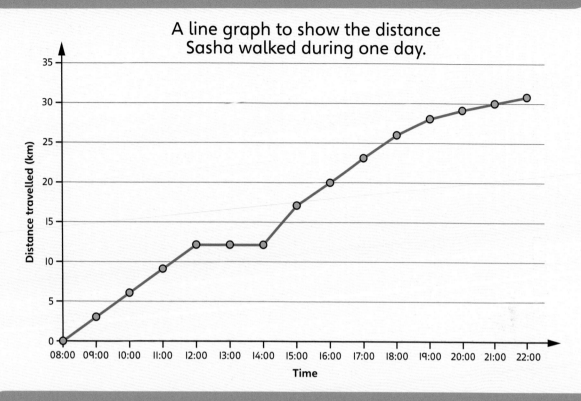

A line graph to show the distance Sasha walked during one day.

Distance travelled (km) (y-axis: 0, 5, 10, 15, 20, 25, 30, 35)

Time (x-axis: 08:00, 09:00, 10:00, 11:00, 12:00, 13:00, 14:00, 15:00, 16:00, 17:00, 18:00, 19:00, 20:00, 21:00, 22:00)

How far had Sasha walked by:

1 12 pm?   **2** 4 pm?   **3** 10 pm?

At what time did she reach:

4 5 km?   **5** 20 km?   **6** 25 km?

7 At what time did she stop for a rest and how long did she stop for?

8 How long did it take her to walk 10 km?

9 Between which two times was she walking the fastest?

10 Between which two times was she walking the slowest but still moving?

THINK Draw a graph for a marathon runner who runs 26 miles in four hours. Do you think they will run the whole marathon at the same speed?

I am confident with reading and interpreting line graphs.

This graph shows approximate conversions from litres to pints.

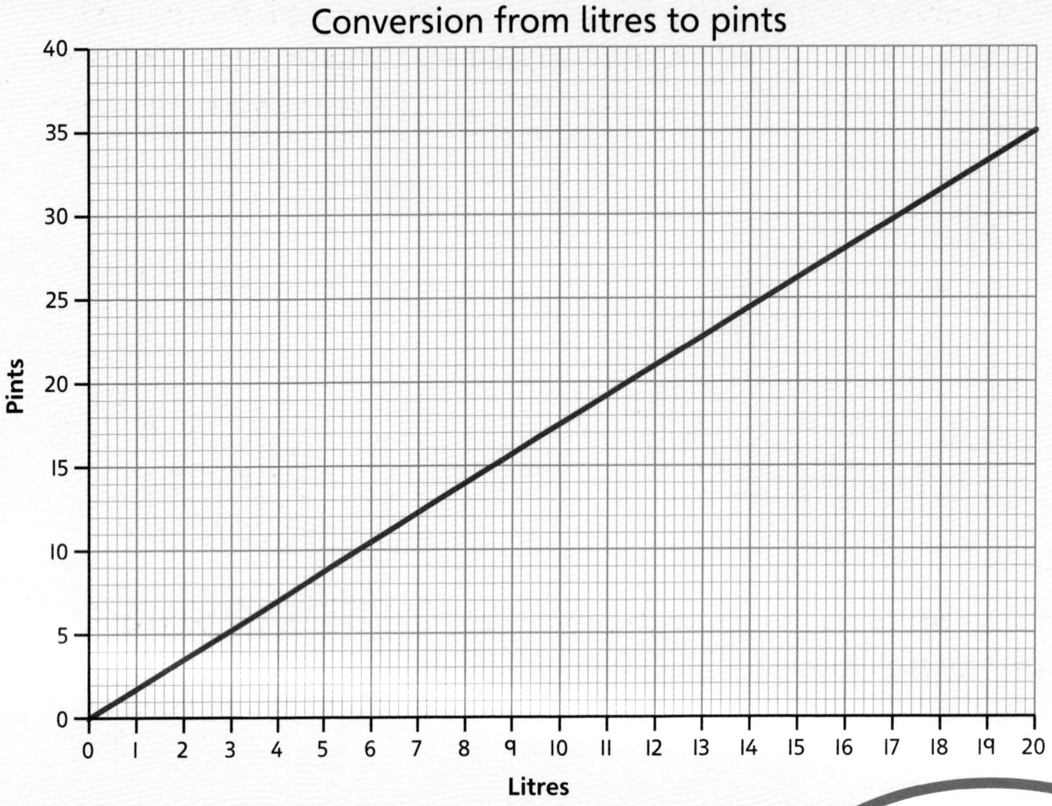

About how many pints in each of these?

1. 10 litres
2. 3 litres
3. 12 litres
4. 18 litres
5. 15 litres
6. 25 litres

1 litre is approximately 1·76 pints. Write your answers to the nearest whole number or nearest tenth.

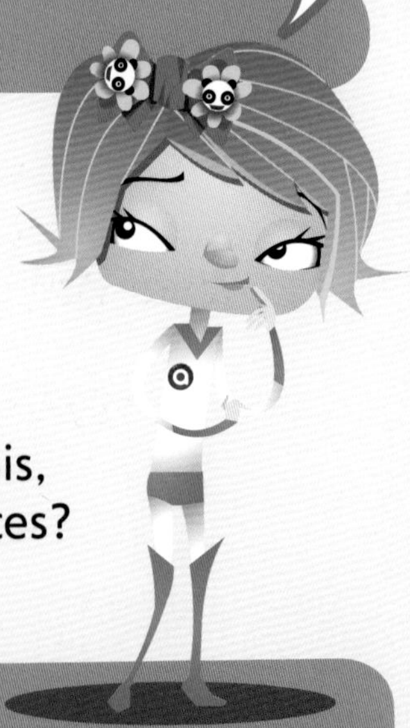

About how many litres in each of these?

7. 3 pints
8. 8 pints
9. 10 pints
10. 20 pints
11. 12 pints
12. 30 pints

THINK

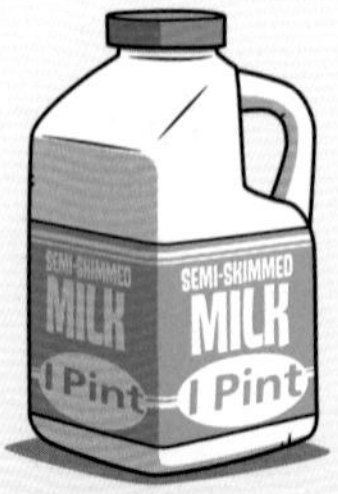

How many litres of milk is this, labelled to two decimal places?

I am confident with reading and interpreting line graphs.

Reading pie charts

Each pie chart shows the results of a survey of a class of 24 children. The survey asked them to choose their favourite day out. Compare the pie charts and answer the questions.

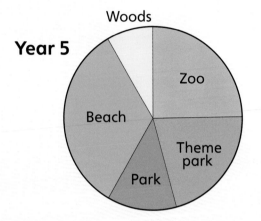

Estimate how many children in Year 5 said their favourite day out was:

1 the zoo   **2** the beach   **3** the park

Estimate how many children in Year 6 said their favourite day out was:

4 the woods   **5** the zoo   **6** the theme park

7 Estimate how many more children in Year 6 than in Year 5 chose the woods as their favourite?

8 Approximately how many children in total chose the beach?

9 Draw a pie chart to show the information in this table. Give your pie chart a title. What do you think it might show?

Swimming	Climbing	Running	Cycling
45%	10%	20%	25%

○ **I am confident with reading and interpreting pie charts.**
○
○

The pie charts show the results of two surveys. Sixty people were asked their favourite genre of book, then eighty were asked their favourite genre of film.

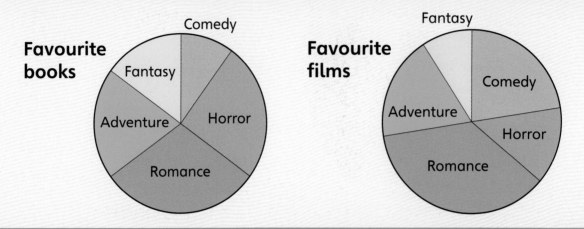

Favourite books

Favourite films

Estimate how many people said their favourite book genre was:

1. comedy

2. horror

3. fantasy

Estimate how many said their favourite film genre was:

4. romance

5. adventure

6. horror

7. Estimate how many more people chose horror as their favourite book genre than chose horror as their favourite film genre?

True or false? Explain your answers.

8. More people chose comedy as their favourite film genre than chose comedy as their favourite book genre.

9. The same number of people chose adventure as their favourite film genre as chose horror as their favourite book genre.

A different group were asked about their least favourite genre of film. Put the results into a pie chart.

10.

Comedy	Horror	Romance	Adventure	Fantasy
20%	15%	10%	30%	25%

I am confident with reading and interpreting pie charts.

Different colours of cars

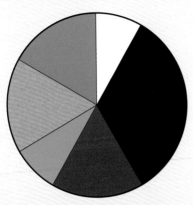

120 cars were surveyed

Estimate what proportion of cars surveyed were:

1. white?

2. blue?

3. green?

4. black?

5. red or green?

6. white or black?

7. not blue or green?

8. one of the colours of the rainbow?

Estimate how many cars were:

9. red?

10. black?

11. silver or white?

12. green or blue?

13. red or white?

14. yellow?

 This chart shows favourite drinks. Discuss with a partner what each slice might represent, for example, pink = juice. If 16 friends were surveyed, how many would be in each category?

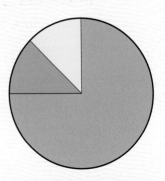

● I am confident with reading and interpreting pie charts.

75

This pie chart shows how 60 children from Hillside School get to school.

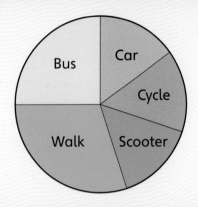

Answer these questions and compare the pie charts.

1. This table shows how 50 children from Lakeside School get to school. Draw a pie chart to show this data and complete the table.

	Number of chn	% of total chn
Bus	7	
Walk	3	
Cycle	12	
Scooter	2	
Car	26	

2. How many more children walk to Hillside School than get the bus?

3. How many more children ride their scooter to Hillside School than ride to Lakeside School?

4. How many more children walk to Hillside School than walk to Lakeside School?

5. How many more children cycle to Lakeside School than cycle to Hillside School?

6. How many more children come by car to Lakeside School than come by car to Hillside School?

○ I am confident with creating and interpreting pie charts.
○
○

Reading coordinates and translating shapes

GRAB! Blank graph paper

Look at the grid below and follow the instructions.

Draw these polygons on your own grid to make them clearer.

① Look at the polygons above. Write the coordinates of each.

② Each polygon is moved two squares to the left. Write the new coordinates of each.

③ After moving to the left, each polygon is now moved two squares up. Write the new coordinates of each.

Decide if these statements are true or false.

④ A square has three corners with coordinates (2, 2), (2, 6), (6, 6). The fourth corner must be (6, 2).

⑤ The vertices of a triangle are (1, 4), (4, 4) and (6, 4).

⑥ In a rectangle, two of the vertices must have the same x-coordinate, and two of the vertices must have the same y-coordinate.

⑦ A parallelogram with vertices (−2, −2), (−3, −5), (−7, −2) and (−8, −5) is moved two squares up the grid. The coordinates of two vertices now have 0 as their x-coordinate.

○ **I am confident with reading coordinates and translating shapes.**

Look at the grid and follow the instructions.

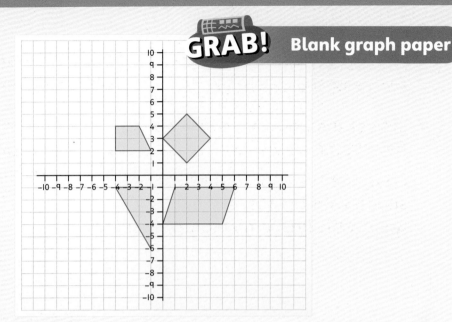

GRAB! **Blank graph paper**

1. Copy each polygon onto your own four-quadrant graph.

2. Write the coordinates of the vertices.

3. Add or subtract six to the x- or y-coordinates to move each shape into a new quadrant. Write the new coordinates.

Answer these questions about coordinates.

4. A rectangle has vertices (3, 2), (7, 2) and (3, 8). Write the missing coordinate.

5. A right-angled triangle has vertices (1, 2), (6, 2) and ($\square$, 6). What are the two possible x-coordinates for the third point?

6. The vertices of a square are: (1, −4), (6, −4), (6, −9) and (a, b). Find the value of a and b.

7. A trapezium has vertices: (−8, 3), (−1, 3) (−7, 7) and (−2, m). Find a value for m.

THINK After one horizontal translation, the coordinates of a triangle are (5, −1), (5, −6) and (8, −6). Before translation, one of its sides ran along the y-axis. What were the coordinates of its vertices then?

Look at the shapes on this grid. Start with shape a and follow the instructions.

1 List the coordinates of each vertex of the polygon.

 **GRAB!** **Blank graph paper**

2 Reflect the polygon in the y-axis. Reflect the new shape in the x-axis.

3 Compare the coordinates of the final shape with the first shape. Which quadrants has it moved from and to?

Draw these polygons on your own grid.

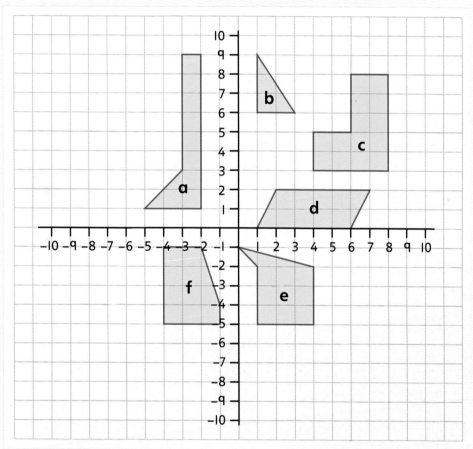

 THINK Write some rules to explain what happens if you change the signs of the numbers in each pair of coordinates representing the vertices of a polygon.

○ **I am confident with reflecting shapes.**
○
○

Calculating angles

Remember angles on a line add to 180° and opposite angles are equal.

Work out the missing angles.

1
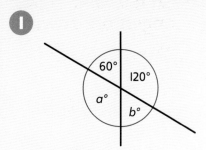
60°
120°
a°
b°

3
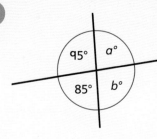
95° a°
85° b°

2
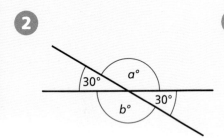
30° a°
b° 30°

4
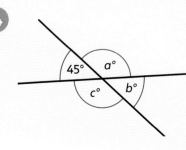
45° a°
c° b°

Work out the missing angles in these triangles.

5
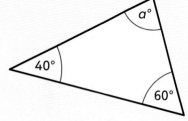
a°
40°
60°

7
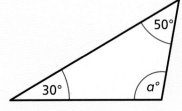
50°
30° a°

6
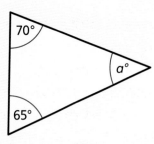
70°
a°
65°

8
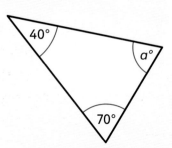
40°
a°
70°

 **THINK** There are three angles on a straight line. The first is 120°. The second is 10° less than the third angle. What size are these two angles?

- I am confident with working out missing angles on
- straight lines and in triangles.

80

Work out the missing angles in each question.

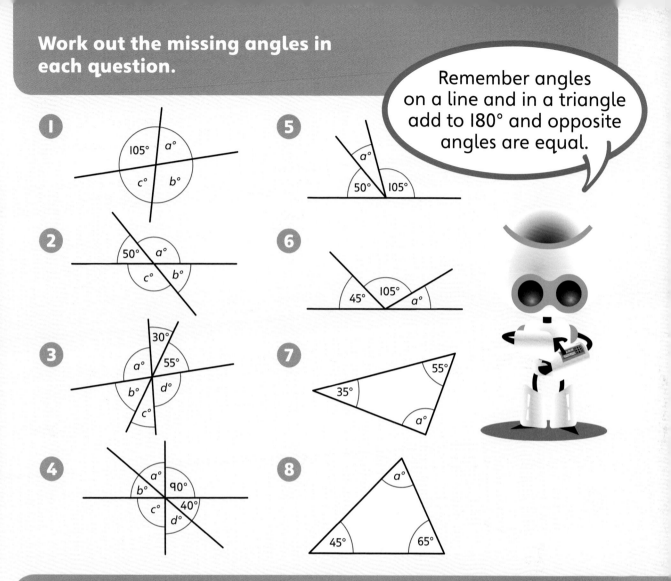

Remember angles on a line and in a triangle add to 180° and opposite angles are equal.

1. 105° a° c° b°

2. 50° a° c° b°

3. 30° 55° a° d° b° c°

4. a° 90° b° c° 40° d°

5. a° 50° 105°

6. 45° 105° a°

7. 55° 35° a°

8. a° 45° 65°

Complete the challenge.

9.

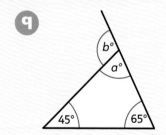

b° a° 45° 65°

Add the two angles given. Write their total.
Use this to find missing angle a.
Use angle a to find missing angle b.
Compare the size of angle b with the total you got when you added the two given angles.

Repeat this for the second triangle.

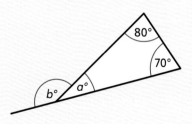

80° 70° b° a°

Now draw a triangle of your own and see if this works. You will need to use a protractor to measure the angles.

I am confident with working out missing angles on straight lines and in triangles.

Work out the missing angles in each question.

1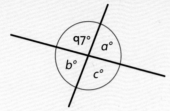

2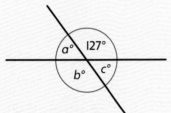

3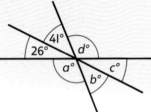

4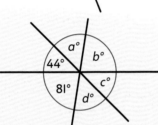

5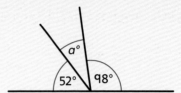

6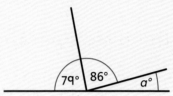

7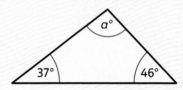

8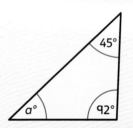

Complete the challenge.

9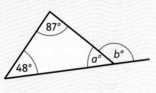

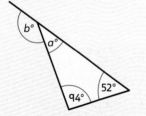

Add the two angles given. Write their total. Use this to find missing angle a.
Use angle a to find the exterior angle, b.
Compare the size of angle b with the total you got when you added the two given angles.

Repeat this for the second triangle.

Now draw a triangle of your own and see if this works. You will need to use a protractor to measure the angles.

I am confident with working out missing angles on straight lines and in triangles.

Solving decimal multiplication problems

Perform these multiplications.

① £5637 × 3 = ☐

③ £2436 × 7 = ☐

② £4 × 7242 = ☐

④ 8365 × 8p = ☐

Solve these multiplication problems.

⑤ A car salesman has four cars for sale at £4859 each. He sells them all, but gives each buyer a £200 discount. How much money does he get in total?

⑥ It costs a printing company 3p per leaflet to print 4518 leaflets. The company then sells them at 8p per leaflet. How much money do they make?

Perform these multiplications.

⑦ £57·42 × 3 = ☐

⑨ £83·77 × 6 = ☐

⑧ 8 × £63·34 = ☐

⑩ £48·19 × 7 = ☐

Solve these problems, which involve multiplying decimals.

⑪ A head teacher buys 9 chairs for the staffroom. Each chair costs £18·57. How much less than £200 does she pay?

⑫ Which costs more and by how much: three jackets at £27·36 each, or five T-shirts at £19·37 each?

THINK Which digits would make this multiplication correct?

6 × ☐ 45 ☐ = 14 742

○ **I am confident with multiplying 4-digit numbers and**
○ **2-place decimals by 1-digit numbers.**

Look at the table and solve the problems.

1 The table shows sales in a hospital shop over two weeks. Work out how much money was made in total each week.

Item	Price	Sales, week 1	Sales, week 2
Wash kit	£12·45	6	5
Headphones	£11·36	9	8
Hospital magazine	£3·65	10	12
E-book reader	£79·25	2	3
Pyjamas	£24·54	6	3
Nightdress	£18·72	4	5
Crossword puzzle book	£4·83	8	9

2 20% of the total each week goes to the hospital as profit. How much is this each week?

3 Which week was more profitable for the hospital? By how much?

○ **I am confident with multiplying decimal numbers in a money context.**

Work out the answers to these multiplications.

The height of this house is 9·23 m. Find the height of:

1 85 houses

2 46 houses

3 55 houses

9·23 m

85 × 9·23 m	85 × 923 cm		
×	900	20	3
80			
5			

Remember to divide the total by 100 at the end.

Complete the sentences.

Taipei 101
509 m

Petronas Towers
452 m

Burj Khalifa
828 m

4 46 houses are about the same height as _____.

5 55 houses are about the same height as _____.

6 85 houses are about the same height as _____.

Perform these multiplications.

7 23 × 26·74 m = ☐

8 26 × 23·65 m = ☐

9 34 × 26·54 m = ☐

10 43 × 53·31 m = ☐

THINK
Arrange the digits 1–5 in a £ ☐☐ · ☐☐ × ☐ multiplication so as to get the smallest possible answer. Use each digit only once.

● I am confident with multiplying decimal numbers
○
○ in measures.

85

Freya is practising for a fun run. Work out how far she runs each time.

1 Garden perimeter 24·37 m

14 laps of the garden

3 Playground perimeter 45·25 m

26 laps of the playground

2 Field perimeter 62·45 m

22 laps of the field

4 5-a-side pitch perimeter 84·52 m

15 laps of the pitch

Work out how much is earned each time.

Write the amount in pence then divide by 100 to give your answer in pounds.

5 £12·37 / hour
for 23 hours

7 £22·44 / hour
for 27 hours

6 £16·25 / hour
for 16 hours

8 £18·76 / hour
for 19 hours

 A snail typically moves at a speed of 1 mm per second. How far could a snail crawl in a fortnight, in metres?

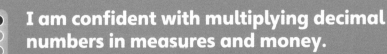

I am confident with multiplying decimal numbers in measures and money.

Perform these multiplications.

1 57·38 m × 24 = ☐

2 17·43 m × 28 = ☐

3 46·37 m × 26 = ☐

4 £75·22 × 32 = ☐

5 £69·37 × 34 = ☐

6 £35·27 × 29 = ☐

7 11·13 × 38 = ☐

8 38·42 × 39 = ☐

9 78·47 × 36 = ☐

10 59·47 × 33 = ☐

11 39·53 × 37 = ☐

12 55·55 × 28 = ☐

13 37·73 × 37 = ☐

14 89·47 × 45 = ☐

 Is it true that if the number of pence in the amount being multiplied is even, then no matter what you multiply it by, the answer will always have an even number of pence?

○ **I am confident with multiplying 2-place decimal numbers.**

87

1 **Divide each of these numbers by 14 and by 24.**

Use these lists of multiples of 14 and 24 to help you.

14	24
28	48
42	72
56	96
70	120
84	144
98	168
112	192
126	216
140	240

2 196 ÷ 14 = ☐

3 360 ÷ 24 = ☐

4 294 ÷ 14 = ☐

5 552 ÷ 24 = ☐

6 350 ÷ 14 = ☐

7 576 ÷ 14 = ☐

 THINK

☐☐☐ ÷ 2☐

Fill in the missing numbers so that the answer is between 20 and 30.

● I am confident with dividing 3-digit numbers by 2-digit numbers.

Use long division to perform these calculations.

Divide each spaceship number by:

1 17

2 23

3 28

$\square\square\square\square \div 2\square$

Fill in the missing numbers so that the answer is between 300 and 400.

○ **I am confident with dividing 4-digit numbers by 2-digit numbers.**

Use long division to perform these calculations.

1. $4637 \div 27 = \square$

2. $7522 \div 31 = \square$

3. $1748 \div 23 = \square$

4. $5738 \div 38 = \square$

5. $6937 \div 32 = \square$

6. $1743 \div 24 = \square$

7. $3842 \div 26 = \square$

8. $7847 \div 36 = \square$

9. $5739 \div 37 = \square$

10. $3527 \div 29 = \square$

11. $7947 \div 34 = \square$

12. $1113 \div 28 = \square$

13. $6213 \div 29 = \square$

14. $5708 \div 19 = \square$

15. A cricketer goes on tour and scores 2416 runs over 16 games. If he scored the same in every game, how many runs did he score in each game?

16. Olivia enters a competition to win a jar of sweets. When she wins she decides to share the jar with her class. There are 4569 sweets in the jar and a total of 27 children in the class. How many sweets do they each get? If the sweets are shared equally and Olivia gets any spare sweets, how many does she get?

There are 52 weeks in a year.

THINK Ibraheem says that his grandfather has been alive for 4680 weeks. He wants to know how old he is in years. Help Ibraheem to find out how many years his grandfather has been alive for.

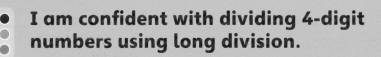

- I am confident with dividing 4-digit numbers using long division.

90

Use long division to perform these calculations.

1 5392 ÷ 24 = ☐

4 2153 ÷ 27 = ☐

2 6948 ÷ 23 = ☐

5 4616 ÷ 29 = ☐

3 1634 ÷ 26 = ☐

6 5738 ÷ 28 = ☐

Solve these word problems.

7 There are 16 ounces in a pound. How many pounds is the same as 4528 ounces?

8 There are 5784 bottles in a factory. They are put into crates with 24 bottles in each crate. How many full crates are there?

9 A cricketer scored 5626 runs over his career at an average of 29 runs a match. How many matches did he play?

10 There are 14 pounds in a stone. How many stones is the same as 7168 pounds?

- I am confident with dividing 4-digit numbers using long division.

Describing functions

Write what each pair of machines is doing. Then write the missing output. Write four more inputs and outputs for each.

1

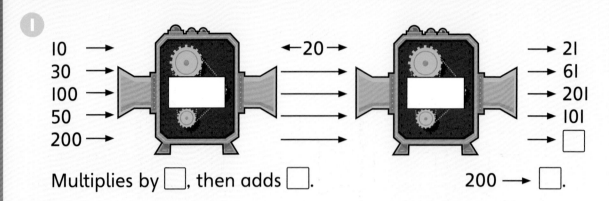

```
10  →          ←20→          → 21
30  →                        → 61
100 →                        → 201
50  →                        → 101
200 →                        → ☐
```

Multiplies by ☐, then adds ☐.   200 → ☐.

2

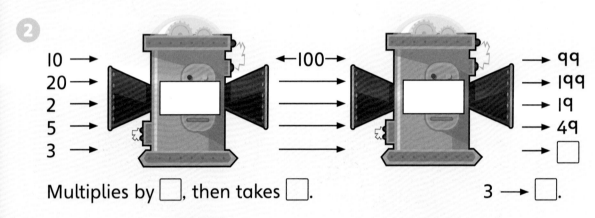

```
10 →          ←100→          → 99
20 →                         → 199
2  →                         → 19
5  →                         → 49
3  →                         → ☐
```

Multiplies by ☐, then takes ☐.   3 → ☐.

3

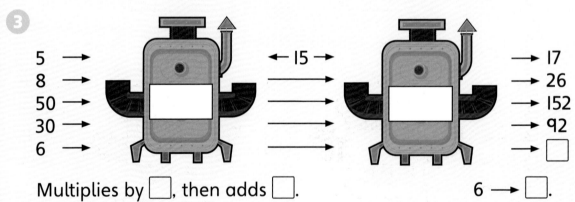

```
5  →          ←15→          → 17
8  →                        → 26
50 →                        → 152
30 →                        → 92
6  →                        → ☐
```

Multiplies by ☐, then adds ☐.   6 → ☐.

THINK — Write your own pair of function machines with three inputs and outputs.

● I am confident with working out the relationship
between numbers in a function machine.

Match each algebraic expression to one of the function machines below. Then write the missing steps for each function machine.

1 10 × n − 5
(10n − 5)

2 5 × n + 2
(5n + 2)

3 4 × n + 10
(4n + 10)

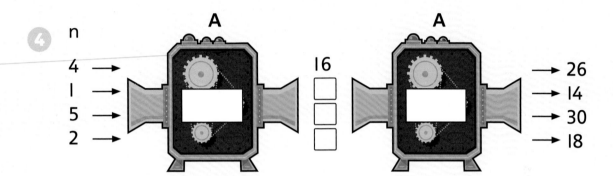

4 n

A
4 →
1 →
5 →
2 →

16

A
→ 26
→ 14
→ 30
→ 18

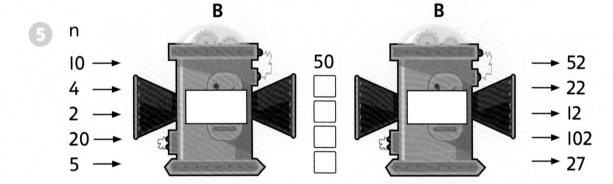

5 n

B
10 →
4 →
2 →
20 →
5 →

50

B
→ 52
→ 22
→ 12
→ 102
→ 27

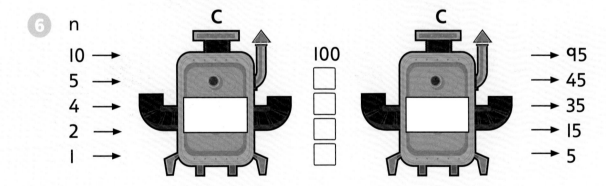

6 n

C
10 →
5 →
4 →
2 →
1 →

100

C
→ 95
→ 45
→ 35
→ 15
→ 5

 If each pair of function machines were put in reverse order so that they added or subtracted first, then multiplied, would the outputs be the same?

● I am confident with working out the relationship
⋮ between numbers in a function machine.

Describe what each pair of function machines is doing, first in words and then using *n*. Then fill in the missing steps.

1

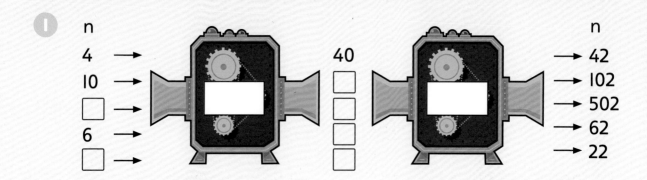

n
4 →
10 →
☐ →
6 →
☐ →

40
☐
☐
☐
☐

n
→ 42
→ 102
→ 502
→ 62
→ 22

2

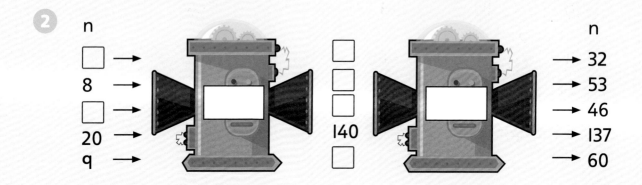

n
☐ →
8 →
☐ →
20 →
9 →

☐
☐
☐
140
☐

n
→ 32
→ 53
→ 46
→ 137
→ 60

3

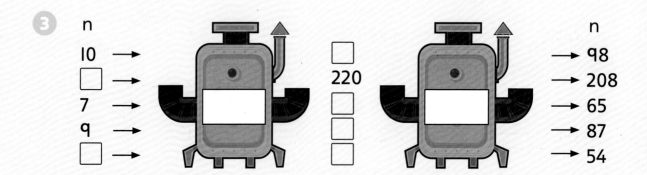

n
10 →
☐ →
7 →
9 →
☐ →

☐
220
☐
☐
☐

n
→ 98
→ 208
→ 65
→ 87
→ 54

4 Write three more inputs and outputs for each machine.

 Draw your own pair of function machines with three inputs and outputs and describe what they do using *n*.

I am confident with working out the relationship between numbers in a function machine.

Describing number sequences

What is the tenth number in each of these sequences?

1. 5   10   15   20   25

2. 4   9   14   19   24

3. 3   13   23   33   43

4. 25   50   75   100   125

5. 10   19   28   37   46

6. 21   41   61   81   101

7. $\frac{1}{4}$ $\frac{1}{2}$ $\frac{3}{4}$ 1 $1\frac{1}{4}$

8. 1·1   1·6   2·1   2·6   3·1

9. 1   8   15   22   29

10. 0·7   1·2   1·7   2·2   2·7

11. 4   15   26   37   48

12. 0·6   0·9   1·2   1·5   1·8

13. $1\frac{1}{2}$ 2 $2\frac{1}{2}$ 3 $3\frac{1}{2}$

14. 15   30   45   60   75

THINK   Choose a sequence. Write how someone could work out the 100th number.

● I am confident with finding patterns in number sequences
and working out later numbers.

Write the next two numbers in each sequence. Then predict the tenth number. In words, write the rule that you must follow to predict any number in the sequence.

1. 11   21   31   41   51

2. 7   12   17   22   27

3. 9   19   29   39   49

4. 13   23   33   43   53

Copy and complete each table. Write each rule using *n*.

5. Rule: Double the number, add 3.

1	2	3	4	5	6	7	8	9	10
5	7								

6. Rule: Multiply by 4, add 1.

1	2	3	4	5	6	7	8	9	10
5				21					

7. Rule: Multiply by 5, subtract 2.

1	2	3	4	5	6	7	8	9	10
3					28				

● I am confident with finding patterns in number sequences and working out later numbers.

Write the next two numbers in each sequence.

1.   2   7   17   37   77
2.   5   6   9   18   45

Copy and complete each table. Write each rule using n.

3. Rule: Double the number, add 13.

1	2	3	4	5	6	7	8	9	10
15	17								

4. Rule: Multiply by 3, add 9.

1	2	3	4	5	6	7	8	9	10
12		18							

5. Rule: Multiply by 6, subtract 6.

1	2	3	4	5	6	7	8	9	10
0					30				

Write the first six numbers and the 10th number in each sequence using the rule given.

6. $3n + 2$

1	2	3	4	5	6	...	10
						...	

7. $5n - 2$

1	2	3	4	5	6	...	10
						...	

● ○ ○ ○   **I am confident with finding patterns in number sequences and working out later numbers.**

Identifying ratios

Write the ratio of patterned tiles to plain tiles.

1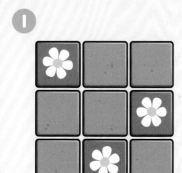

3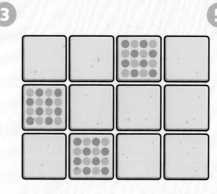

5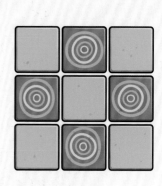

2

4

If the ratio of blue to orange tiles is 3:5, write the number of orange tiles in each of these sets.

6 16 tiles   **7** 40 tiles   **8** 800 tiles

9 Becky makes some squash. It is made with one part squash to five parts water. She uses 50 ml of squash. How many millilitres of water does she need?

THINK Write four pairs of numbers. Each pair should have a ratio of 3:1.

○ **I am confident with identifying ratios.**
○
○

Answer the questions about the picture below.

Write the ratio of children for each of the following. Write the ratios in their simplest form where possible.

1. plain tops: patterned tops
2. striped tops: spotted tops
3. hats: no hats
4. striped tops: plain tops
5. spotted tops: plain tops

Solve these ratio problems.

6. A box has milk and dark chocolates. The ratio of milk to dark is 3:4. If there are 21 chocolates altogether in the box, how many are milk chocolates and how many are dark chocolates?

7. A male tennis player has a win:loss ratio of 3:1. If he has won 36 matches, how many has he lost?

8. A female tennis player has won 42 matches and lost 30 matches. What is her win:loss ratio in its simplest form?

 Write four pairs of numbers that have a ratio of 5:2.

word problems

1. Emily has £48·58 in her wallet and £75·87 in her bank account. She uses her money to buy a computer game that costs £111·49. How much money does she have now?

2. Julie decided to go on a cycling holiday. She rode 67·73 miles on the first day. On the second day she rode 86·48 miles. She wants to cover 200 miles in three days. How far does she need to ride on the third day?

3. Each gold and silver medal from an athletics competition weighs 0·41 kg. The bronze medal weighs 0·05 kg less. What is the weight of the medals held by a person who won two gold, one silver and three bronze medals?

4. An air ticket to fly to Dubai costs £628. Is the cost of 23 tickets greater than £12 000? If so, by how much?

5. Jon uses a cycling app. It tells him that he has been on 1774 rides and that he rides, on average, 28 km per ride. What is the overall distance of all his rides and how much further has he got to go to have cycled 50 000 km?

6. Ahmed is a boat painter. In one week he uses 4·36 l of blue paint. He uses 7·28 l more white paint than blue paint. If the blue and white paint costs £3 per litre, how much did he spend on paint?

7. A scientist measures 5·6 ml of acid into a test-tube. With a pipette he carefully takes out 0·37 ml of the acid. Finally he adds 2·09 ml of water into the test-tube. How much liquid is in the test-tube now?

8. A famous footballer earns £7 654 743 in one year. In the following year his income increases by £944 354. How much does he earn in the two years put together?

Practising calculations

1. $1634 \div 26 = \square$

2. $£57.42 \times 3 = \square$

3. $14.86 + 35.48 + 12.57 = \square$

4. $23.18 - 15.04 = \square$

5. $12 \times £458 = \square$

6. $14.7 - 3.2 = \square$

7. $43.49 - 37.77 = \square$

8. $32846 - 1999 = \square$

9. $27.6 - 4.99 = \square$

10. 35% of £60 = $\square$

11. $24\overline{)4675}$

12.
$$\begin{array}{r} 7.6 \\ 1.92 \\ + \quad 1.3 \\ \hline \end{array}$$

13. $16\overline{)5739}$

14. $(14 - 7) \times 7 + 4 = \square$

15.
$$\begin{array}{r} 723717 \\ - \quad 351824 \\ \hline \end{array}$$

16.
$$\begin{array}{r} 3627 \\ \times \quad 13 \\ \hline \end{array}$$

17. $5738 \div 28 = \square$

18. $£83.77 \times 6 = \square$

19. $37.46 - 14.01 = \square$

20. $36.83 + 8.78 = \square$

21. $£367 \times 9 = \square$

22. $47.48 - 10.16 = \square$

23. $50.94 - 38.17 = \square$

24. $312 - 257 = \square$

25. $92 - 67 = \square$

26. 95% of £12 = $\square$

27. $18\overline{)3284}$

28.
$$\begin{array}{r} 4.7 \\ 2.47 \\ + \quad 1.79 \\ \hline \end{array}$$

29. $14\overline{)497}$

30. $54.72 - 8.99 = \square$

31.
$$\begin{array}{r} 9738138 \\ - \quad 2571453 \\ \hline \end{array}$$

32.
$$\begin{array}{r} 5624 \\ \times \quad 26 \\ \hline \end{array}$$

Algebra puzzles

Three children play tennis. They are all different ages.

When Rory and Sam play each other the total of their ages is 24.

When Tom and Sam play each other the total of their ages is 19.

When Tom and Rory play each other the total of their ages is 21.

1. Who you think is the oldest? Explain why you think that is.

2. Who do you think is the youngest?

3. Use the letter R to stand for Rory's age, the letter S to stand for Sam's age and the letter T to stand for Tom's age. Write three additions (one for each statement above) to show the information you know.

4. Use your first and second additions to help you work out how many years older Rory is than Tom.

5. Use your second and third additions to help you work out how many years older Rory is than Sam.

6. Now write their names in order of age, starting with the oldest. Write the age differences between them.

7. Can you work out how old each person is? Remember to use the information you have found out. Compare the different additions. You could even add together or subtract the additions to find new information.

   Rory's age = ☐   Sam's age = ☐   Tom's age = ☐

8. Check that each statement above is true for the ages you have found.

9. What is the total of all three children's ages?

Four adults play tennis. The adults are all different ages.

> When Amy and Ben play each other the total of their ages is 80.
> When Clio and Ben play each other the total of their ages is 100.
> When Clio and Dan play each other the total of their ages is 75.
> When Ben and Dan play each other the total of their ages is 95.

10. Use the letters A, B, C and D to stand for the ages of the adults. Write four additions (one for each statement above) to show the information you know.

11. Use your first and second additions to help you work out whether Amy is older or younger than Clio and by how many years.

12. Use your second and third additions to help you work out whether Ben is older or younger than Dan and by how many years.

13. Use your third and fourth to help you work out whether Ben is older or younger than Clio and by how many years.

14. Now write their names in order of age, starting with the oldest. Write the age differences between them.

15. Can you work out how old each person is? Remember to use the information you have found out.

    Amy's age = ☐ Ben's age = ☐ Clio's age = ☐ Dan's age = ☐

16. Check that each statement above is true for the ages you have found.

17. What is the total of all four adults' ages?

18. Choose three or four names of people and their ages. Make up a similar puzzle for a partner to solve.

Series Editor
Ruth Merttens

Author Team
Jennie Kerwin and Hilda Merttens

Published by Pearson Education Limited, Edinburgh Gate, Harlow, Essex, CM20 2JE.

www.pearsonschools.co.uk

Text © Pearson Education Limited 2014
Page design and layout by room9design
Original illustrations © Pearson Education Limited 2014
Illustrated by Marek Jagucki pp9, 27, 29, 32, 40, 48–49, 60–61, 65–68, 70, 72, 83, 85–86, 88–89, 91, 98–99;
Matt Buckley pp20–22, 35–38, 41, 62–64, 69–82; Andrew Painter pp92–94; Villie Karabatzia pp33
Cover design by Pearson Education Limited
Cover illustration and Abacus character artwork by Volker Beisler © Pearson Education Limited
Additional contributions by Hilary Koll and Steve Mills, CME Projects Ltd.
First published 2014

16
10 9 8 7 6 5 4

British Library Cataloguing in Publication Data
A catalogue record for this book is available from the British Library

ISBN 978 1 408 27857 4

Printed in Slovakia

Acknowledgements
We would like to thank the staff and pupils at North Kidlington Primary School, Haydon Wick Primary School, Swindon, St Mary's Catholic Primary School, Bodmin, St Andrew's C of E Primary & Nursery School, Sutton-in-Ashfield, Saint James' C of E Primary School, Southampton and Harborne Primary School, Birmingham, for their invaluable help in the development and trialling of this book.

Every effort has been made to contact copyright holders of material reproduced in this book. Any omissions will be rectified in subsequent printings if notice is given to the publishers.